PERFECTION
COLLIDES
WITH FREE WILL

What Genesis, Jesus & his apostles
teach about being male & female
in a troubled world

Gary A. Williams

SNO Publishing
Washougal, WA
Revised 2019

PERFECTION *COLLIDES* WITH FREE WILL

www.snopublishing.com
Address correspondence to:
info@snopublishing.com

Print ISBN: 978-0-578-52535-8

Library of Congress Control Number: 2019907272

Epub ISBN: 978-0-578-52561-7

Contents

For a FREE teacher / discussion leader guide,
go to www.snopublishing.com

Acknowledgments

My long-time interest in what the Bible says about the topics covered in this book is owed in large part to outstanding teachers, such as Dr. S. Scott Bartchy, author and professor, who served as founder and director of UCLA's Center for the Study of Religion; Dr. Gary Tiffin, author, professor and long-time dean at Pacific Christian College; and Dr. David Root, also a professor, author and seminar presenter. I met them through a ministry I helped to found – a ministry that sponsored workshops and seminars by all three in the 1970s.

Their insights contrasted with what my wife, Raelene, and I had been taught previously, and caused us to dig deeper into the Bible on our own. I believe this study, early in our marriage, helped us forge a happy partnership that has now lasted more than half a century.

Owners of small businesses may be encouraged to know that as owner-managers of a successful design and manufacturing company in Silicon Valley, we shared six-day workweeks and 10-hour days for about half of those years – and we're still happily married.

Selling our business and moving into retirement provided me with the opportunity to return to my early roots as a writer and editor. During this new time of life, I've greatly appreciated the patience of friends and family as I've asked them to look at one draft after another of this Genesis paper that grew into a small book.

Among those who have read my text and offered encouragement along the way are: Dr. Stan Johnson, who was our pastor at Saratoga Federated Church in California; Dr. Bryce Jessup, president emeritus of William Jessup University in Rocklin, California, and our pastor at a key point in our lives; Dr. David Timms, the dean of the Faculty of Theology/School of Christian Leadership at William Jessup University; and our friend and pastor in Washington state, Jake Hendrix, an exceptionally gifted teacher who holds a master's degree in applied theology.

I also appreciate the encouragement of Fritz Ridenour, author and editor of dozens of books and articles on faith, who I met while working in publishing in the 1970s and reconnected with via email decades later.

Special thanks go to Dina Hovde, journalist and friend, whose editing of my text proved, once again, that this author should never attempt to final-proof his own work.

Others who have encouraged and assisted include: Laura Casey Elliott, Ron Moen, Jim Leverich, Jeff Ehli, Doug Quinn, Mary Jensen and Sherry Bradley. I am also grateful for the men and women I've spent many hours with in two evening Bible studies. Their friendship and biblical insights are more valuable than I can express.

Last, and most important, thanks go to Raelene. She always comes up with a question or comment to put me on the right track.

Gary Williams

Introduction

The first chapter in most books is designed to draw readers into the story and set a foundation for what comes next. As the first book in the Bible, Genesis has the same function. Those who skip Genesis or who, in effect, only glance at the well-known word pictures (Adam & Eve in the garden, a serpent that talks, God wandering among the fruit trees and shrubs, etc.), are like people who walk into a movie after several key scenes have played and spend the rest of the show trying to figure out the plot.

Genesis is usually thought of as a book about origins. It is really about purpose and relationship. In the first three chapters of Genesis we are introduced to the God of the universe, the world He created, the humans He created, how He designed us to live in relationship with one another and the role He gave us as caretakers of the Earth. Here, at the beginning of recorded time, we discover that humans and animals lived in harmony, that God himself walked among them and that God and humans enjoyed fellowship with one another as naturally as if between a parent and his much-loved children. Then, the story takes a dramatic turn and things go terribly wrong.

I've read Genesis numerous times throughout my life and thought I knew it well. It was a surprise to find out how little I really understood until I immersed myself in a thorough study of the text. For me, these thought-provoking chapters not only reinforce my trust in God, but help me find handles for explaining why the world is how it is, how God intended it to be and what His plan is for the future.

I have done my best to unpack what is in the text, while being mindful of my personal biases and the biases of others. I have also included New Testament Scriptures about Jesus and his apostles, to expand the discussion of male-female roles that begins in the first three chapters of Genesis. I can't think of a better starting point than Genesis 1-3 to learn about God's design for men and women.

"I praise God for science ... *the 'reconciliation' of science and the Bible is a serious task, because they are both so fundamental to humankind's call to be responsible children of God." — Allure of Gentleness,* by Dallas Willard, philosopher and theologian

"The necessary precondition for the birth of science as we know it is, it would seem, the diffusion through society of the belief that the universe is both rational and contingent. Such a belief is the presupposition of modern science and cannot by any conceivable argument be a product of science. One has to ask: Upon what is this belief founded?" — The Gospel in a Pluralist Society, by Lesslie Newbigin, theologian and author

---

Learning how to read Genesis

There are two common misconceptions that affect how readers understand Genesis. The first has to do with trying to use the Bible as a science textbook. Theologian Francis Schaeffer points out in his book, *Genesis in Space and Time,* that the Bible gives us true knowledge, but not exhaustive knowledge. This is an important distinction.

If someone is looking for the Bible to answer all their scientific questions, they will be disappointed. The Bible's authors do not attempt to present exhaustive knowledge about creation or any other process subject to scientific study. Instead, they give us what is necessary if we are to step into the intersection of this world and God's to meet our Creator.

A second misconception has to do with the current cultural conceit which holds that the men and women who came centuries before us were intellectually primitive and, generally, less intelligent than we are today. A quick cruise across the Internet reveals that today's supposedly superior minds still worship a wide variety of conflicting gods, follow occult practices similar to those in ancient times and continue to live the same types of destructive lifestyles that made life difficult in the earliest times. Cruelty, greed, rape, sexual slavery, economic slavery, adultery, misuse of power, racism and discrimination are still part of our world today, just as they were when Genesis was written.

It's a mistake to think we moderns are more intelligent because we have access to massive amounts of information not available in ancient times. Old Testament men and women were a mixture of smart and not so smart, kind and cruel, just as we find in our society. It should be obvious that access to both knowledge and lessons from the past do not guarantee either will be used wisely or for the greater good.

Are science and the Bible mutually exclusive?

There was a time when Genesis was widely accepted as a history of the first years of creation. In our current culture, however, science is king and, for many, the theory of contingent evolution (evolution by accident) overrules even the possibility that a loving God had a hand in creation, let alone that He is still involved in life on Earth.

Proponents of evolution by accident claim that science argues against the possibility of God and the realm of the supernatural. As for me, after considering the arguments for and against theism (a belief in one Creator-God who is still actively involved in our world), I am convinced Genesis makes a better case for God as Creator than the scientific view does to prove:

1. "Nothingness" accidentally and instantly became something (matter).

2. Over time, this new unconscious matter evolved from random chaos into a universe of complicated, intertwining, highly consistent "natural laws."

3. Eventually, unconscious matter came alive, became aware of its surroundings and acquired personality.

4. All of the above happened in a closed system, with no outside design or assistance.

Personal observation over decades has shown me that random and unguided do not lead to orderly and consistent. More importantly, I've come to believe there is a spiritual component that can't be rationalized into insignificance because scientists don't know how to test it, let alone how to create a duplicate of a spiritual event in a science lab.

I can't prove scientifically that this spiritual component exists or is from God, but neither can anyone prove the opposite. Because neither I nor any scientist can prove scientifically that God does or doesn't exist, both sides of this argument are based on faith.

Who wrote the book?

Genesis was written about 3,400 years ago by an author who understood the difference between fact and fiction, history and myth. This author also had an exceptional mind for science. Either that or he had inside information about the creation process from someone who was there. The book is generally attributed to Moses.

Both Jewish and Christian religious leaders and scholars have held this view from ancient times, though his authorship is now being disputed by some modern theories. If Moses is the author, did God give him the creation account he wrote or did he draw on oral traditions or written histories?

Because Genesis does not explain where his information came from, we can't know for sure, but we do know that God and Moses were in close contact. Exodus 33:11 tells us that God spoke to Moses *"face to face, as one speaks to a friend."* With this type of relationship, it is not only possible that God served as the author's expert fact checker, it is entirely likely. For more about the authorship and authority of Genesis, please see Appendix I at the end of this book.

Should we take what the Bible says "literally"?

This question is unanswerable without specifying which part of the Bible is in question. Literal means, "The taking of words in their usual or most basic sense without metaphor or allegory, or representing the exact words of the original text." As noted, Genesis contains a variety of literary forms. Historical narratives are meant to be taken literally. Poems, songs and metaphors are not.

There's also another consideration. "Literal" implies one is reading the "exact words of the original text." Most of us read the Bible as it has been translated, rather than directly from ancient Hebrew or Greek texts. Translations do not always convey the subtle differences found in the original languages. "Yom," the Hebrew word for day, is an excellent example. If you know that "yom" can mean a solar day or an indeterminate length of time, it opens new possibilities for how to read certain Scriptures. Having a Hebrew-Greek concordance handy is a big help when seeking to understand the Bible. (*Strong's Exhaustive Concordance of the Bible* is one good choice.)

"Like a non-fundamentalist Christian, Jim Chee believed in the poetic metaphor of the Navajo story of human genesis. Without believing in the specific Adam's rib, or the size of the reed through which the Holy People emerged to the Earth Surface World, he believed in the lessons such imagery was intended to teach." — Skinwalkers, by Tony Hillerman, a popular author known for his Navajo Tribal Police mystery novels

Creation "myths" or myth-conceptions?

I believe the first verse of Genesis guides us directly into space-time history. While not every Christian agrees, I also believe my view is reinforced throughout Genesis and in other books of the Bible. For instance, in Chapter 4 of Deuteronomy, when Moses knows he is about to die, he reminds his people of their history. That history includes God's creation of humans, as is told in the first chapters of Genesis.

After Moses dies, Joshua becomes the leader of the Jews. Years later, when Joshua is about to die, he also reminds the people about all that God had done for them and what they had actually seen and heard of God's participation in space-time history (Joshua 23). Moving to the New Testament, when the Apostle John opens his Gospel he acknowledges Jesus as God, the one by whom and through whom the universe was created. John then writes about the actual historical events he personally witnessed while walking with Jesus. This same Jesus referred to events in Genesis and other Old Testament texts as historical fact.

The unity of Genesis 1 and 2

Some modern scholars believe that Genesis teaches us about God using myths drawn from cultures that predated the nation of

Israel. Other scholars express the view that Genesis 1 and 2 are separate books by separate authors that originally stood alone. A third group takes the position that the first two Genesis chapters are complementary pieces that belong together.

One reason to stand in the third camp, as I do, is that Jesus combined the two chapters as a united whole: *"Some Pharisees came to him to test him. They asked, 'Is it lawful for a man to divorce his wife for any and every reason?' 'Haven't you read,' he replied, 'that at the beginning the Creator 'made them male and female,' and said, 'For this reason a man will leave his father and mother and be united to his wife and the two will become one flesh'? So they are no longer two, but one flesh. Therefore, what God has joined together, let no one separate"* (Matthew 19:3-6). The first part of Jesus' statement refers to Genesis 1:27; the second part to Genesis 2:24.

In his book on Genesis, Schaeffer points out that Mark 10:6-8 provides a similar illustration of the unity between Genesis 1 and 2. He writes, "These passages from Mark are tied to one another and form the basis of Jesus' moral standard concerning marriage. Jesus reaches back and puts together the creation of humans in Genesis 1 with the creation of two specific humans in Genesis 2."

Perhaps what is throwing those who fail to see the historicity and unity of Genesis 1 and 2 is the literary structure of the book. The author often introduces an idea briefly before covering it in more detail. Nowhere is this structure more evident than in Genesis 1, which introduces the entire creation, including the first humans, and tells of our special role in the created world. Genesis 2 shines the spotlight directly on humanity and Chapter 3 keeps the focus on humans, describing the first rebellion against God and its consequences.

Regarding those who feel that Genesis 1 and 2 present conflicting information, I like what my friend Jeff Ehli said when

I was struggling with how to write about them. Jeff is a scholar, one who loves heavy theological and philosophical treatises that are full of sentences I struggle to decipher, even with my 20-pound dictionary close at hand.

It was Jeff's concise, clear take on the matter that put me back on track: "I don't see contradictions between Genesis 1 and 2 as a problem. I think we read things in a much more linear way than people did thousands of years ago. If you take away the western modernist mindset the 'contradictions' disappear.

"I think it's mostly because we live in a culture where the written word is so easily accessible. The exact phrasing is much more important when you can write it down or immediately look it up. People in oral cultures relied more on memory. They were less exact with their descriptions of events.

"There's also the issue of what particular theological point the author is trying to draw out. It makes sense that Moses would tell the story one way when he's trying to convey God's sovereignty over creation (Genesis 1) and another way when trying to discuss sin (Genesis 2-3)."

A note about Bible translations

For the sake of consistency in this book, unless otherwise noted, all Bible quotes are from the New International Version (NIV). I also use other translations when they help to clarify verses and/ or bring out meanings that might otherwise be missed.

Genesis Chapter 1

Key thought:

God created. *These two words offer the key to all that follows.*

How God created is not fully explained, but what modern scientists believe to be true about the order of creation is essentially the same as what was written in Genesis 3,400 years ago. Where the wider scientific community differs is in the refusal of many to recognize God in the creation process.

"In the beginning, there was nothing. And then, in an explosive instant: Everything. That explains not just Stanford physicist Andrei Linde's landmark theory, but also his moment of epiphany, in Moscow 30 years ago, that transformed our understanding of the beginnings of the universe. Astronomers announced new findings last week that, if corroborated, validate his pioneering vision that the universe was born in a fraction of a second, expanding exponentially from a size smaller than a proton. Last Monday, a team of scientists reported that a telescope at the South Pole had detected gravitational waves that are the first tremors of the Big Bang, when the universe was a trillionth of a trillionth of a trillionth of a second old. The news, heralded as one of cosmology's biggest discoveries, lends 'smoking gun' evidence to Linde's once-radical Chaotic Inflation theory about the universe's violent expansion." – "Stanford: Big Bang tremors may back physicist's universe-birth theory," *San Jose Mercury News*, March 23, 2014, by Lisa M. Krieger, science writer

---

Current scientific wisdom says that introducing God is
a matter of faith and faith is not pertinent to a discussion of
science. However, scientists routinely develop theories about
the beginnings of our universe they can't prove and defend them
with a faith that shames those of us who call ourselves Christians.
After all, what is the belief that we live in a "contingent" universe
– one created by accident and without cause – other than a
matter of faith?

Genesis 1:1

In the beginning God created the heavens and the earth.

If our universe began with a big bang, God lit the fuse.

The main thrust of Chapters 1 and 2 is that God planned,
created and organized our world. Moses, so far as we know, was
not a scientist, nor did he claim that God gave him access to a
thick, highly detailed owner's manual to explain how the world
works and how to maintain it. My belief is that God wants us to
enjoy the process of discovery as much as He enjoyed the process
of creation. He creates and organizes. We seek to understand how
an already created universe functions. Understanding our world
is absolutely essential if we are to be wise caretakers of what God
has given us.

Comparing ancient Moses to the latest science

As we look for answers about our world and ourselves, we come
to realize that we humans are headstrong creatures who are not
shy about saying what type of God we will or won't believe in.
That being the case, how could the first line of any book hold
a greater meaning than is contained here? *"In the beginning God
created."* This short verse tells us that something existed before
the heavens and the Earth existed, before the beginning of space-
time history. This something – God – is not a nameless, formless

collection of random matter and/or energy floating in space. This one true God has a personality and an ability to create on a scale that is far beyond our human imaginations.

"In the beginning, there was nothing. And then, in an explosive instant: Everything." What impresses me most about Lisa Krieger's 2014 article in the San Jose Mercury News is how well this scientific revelation lines up with the first sentence in the first book of the Bible. When we combine Genesis 1:1 with the big-bang theory, we can logically rewrite the article's lead sentence this way: "In the beginning God was in His space, then, in an explosive instant, He created our space out of nothing."

Ironically, many people will reject my rewrite because they find it difficult to recognize God's role in designing what they consider to be a "natural" process.

"Heaven," meaning God's space and "heavens," meaning the sky

One of the best descriptions I've read of "heaven" comes from N. T. Wright in his wonderful book, *Simply Christian*. He writes that the Bible's authors move easily between using "heavens" to describe where God dwells and using the word to mean a place in our world of space and time (i.e., the sky).

Over time, the word has also come to describe a destination, "The place where God's people will be with him in blissful happiness after they die," says Wright. According to him, this definition came into use "because the word (heaven) offers a way of talking about where God always is, so that the promise held out in the phrase 'going to heaven' is more or less exactly 'going to be with God in the place where he's been all along.'

"Thus 'heaven' is not just a future reality, but a present one." If "heaven," when used to define God's dwelling place, is not meant to describe where God is found in our world, asks Wright,

"How do heaven and Earth, God's space and our space, relate to one another?"

How God's space overlaps our space

Wright illustrates his answer by describing two spheres, one that represents God's spiritual world and the other our world of time, space and matter. The Bible, beginning in the first chapter of Genesis, consistently shows that God's sphere and ours overlap, so that God is seen in and involved in, our space-time world. This understanding regarding the overlap of our world and God's is foundational to Judaism and Christianity.

In *Simply Christian*, Wright also provides an especially helpful explanation regarding the Temple in Jerusalem. The Temple in ancient Israelite belief, he points out, was thought of as where heaven and Earth met, as stated in Psalm 132:13-14: *"For the Lord has chosen Zion, he has desired it for his dwelling, saying, 'This is my resting-place for ever and ever; here will I sit enthroned, for I have desired it.'"*

When pilgrims and worshipers went to Jerusalem and into the Temple to worship and offer sacrifices, he writes, they wouldn't have said they were going into heaven. They would have said they were going to "the place where heaven and Earth overlapped and interlocked."

To a Christ follower, the place where heaven and Earth now meet is Jesus, who referred to his own body as a temple: *"Destroy this temple and I will raise it again in three days"* (John 2:19). It is to Jesus that we go to meet God.

Historical note regarding the Jewish Temple:
King David captured Jerusalem and made it the capital of the Jewish kingdom in about 1000 B.C. The first Jewish Temple – their holiest site – was built there about 986 B.C. It was destroyed in 586 B.C. and a second

Temple was built about 516 B.C. Though that Temple was destroyed in 70 A.D., the site remained holy to the Jews, who longed to rebuild once again. That was not to be. In 610 A.D., about 1,600 years after the first Jewish Temple was built in Jerusalem, Islam was founded. Just a few years later, a massive Muslim army captured Jerusalem.

In 691 A.D. the Muslim captors built a Mosque right on top of where the Jewish Temple used to stand. Much of what is happening in the Middle East today is related to the long-running dispute over who should control Jerusalem and the site that has become holy to two religions.

For more about this time in history and the crusades that followed the Muslim capture of Jerusalem, read, "The Real History of the Crusades," written by Thomas F. Madden for Christianity Today, May 6, 2005.

We see the Great Artist in His creation

In 1961, Yuri Gagarin, a Russian cosmonaut, was the first human to enter outer space. Misunderstanding who God is and how to meet Him, Gagarin famously reported back to Earth: "I see no God up here."

The idea that we can travel far enough out into the heavens and find God's person is not biblical. God's creation, however, is a 24/7 reminder of who He is and what He can do. Gagarin was experiencing the work of the Great Artist every time he looked out the window of his space capsule; Gagarin just didn't realize what he was seeing.

Just as one can learn about a human by looking at his or her creations, we can learn about God by looking at His creation. God gives us an appreciation for beauty, a longing for love and relationship and a desire to understand the spiritual world – His world.

A person who appreciates beauty in the world does so because God appreciates beauty. We love because God loves. We desire relationship because God desires relationship. We desire to know about the spiritual world because that is God's domain. All of the above tells us about the character of our Creator.

He could have created humans as puppets who dance to His manipulations. Instead, He gives us free will, even knowing we will abuse it and lose our way. But God also makes it known that we are welcome back into His presence, despite our rebellious behavior and He makes the path back a matter of grace (undeserved favor), not how we perform for Him.

God willed creation into existence

The author of Hebrews writes in Chapter 11:3: *"By faith we understand that the universe was formed at God's command, so that what is seen was not made out of what was visible."* In 2 Peter 3:5 there is a similar statement: *"By God's word the heavens came into being and the earth was formed out of water and by water."*

The Greek term we translate as "command" or "word" in Hebrews 11:3 is "rhema." It means an utterance, as in a command. In other words, God speaks and it is so. The Greek term for "word" in 2 Peter 3:5 is "logos." It means "said" and includes the meaning of "thought." In this case, Peter is telling us God does not have to speak, but can merely think something into being. Look humans, no hands!

"In the beginning" was only the beginning

God continues to work in human history, as we find throughout the Bible. One such reference is Hebrews 1:1-3: *"In the past God spoke to our ancestors through the prophets at many times and in various ways, but in these last days he has spoken to us by his Son, whom he appointed heir of all things and through whom also he made the universe. The Son is the radiance of God's glory and the exact representation of his being, sustaining all things by his powerful word. After he had provided purification for sins, he sat down at the right hand of the Majesty in heaven.*" History is advancing toward the glory of God. Life has purpose.

The individual Christ follower's view is found in Romans 8:28: "*And we know that in all things God works for the good of those who love him, who have been called according to His purpose.*" God is the foundation upon which we followers of Jesus build our distinctly Christian answer to the questions, "Who am I?" and "Why am I here?"

Those who claim that our human origins are impersonal must deal with at least two major problems: First, there is no real explanation for the fact that our world not only exists but has a specific form and consistent natural laws.

This sort of world is inconsistent with a random, impersonal beginning. Second and more important, if we begin with an impersonal universe there is no explanation for personality. Personality becomes a major issue when we're asking "Who?" and "Why?"

The biblical response to both questions begins with the understanding that humans are God's creations and we are loved by Him. He designed us to love Him, to love one another and to do the work He sets out for us. It is in worshiping and living for God that we find our purpose.

The Bible also explains why humans throughout the world and across the centuries tend to seek love, beauty, justice, peace and an understanding of the spiritual nature that is an essential part of us all. The biblical view even makes clear why these desires are built into the world's major religions, despite differences that often revolve around how we got here and what our purpose is.

The Bible's answer is that we share the same basic desires because God creates all of us in His image. In other words, these desires we hold in common with one another, we also hold in common with our Creator.

Our Western culture is built on a Judeo-Christian tradition that begins with the personal. However, there are many today who are eager to put an arrow through the heart of our "old school" personal God premise and happily paint bullseye targets on anything that smacks of Judeo-Christian heritage.

The replacement, apparently, is to be a culture built on the faith that an impersonal nothing created something out of nothing and that nothingness developed personality over time, all in a closed system (a system with no outside input or control). This happened thanks to consistent natural laws that completely contradict the theory that we live in a world that is random, unplanned and without purpose.

While a random and impersonal beginning cannot explain where the "natural" laws that govern our amazing universe came from – let alone the personality found in women and men – the Bible can and does.

"The unity of the Bible is found in the development of a with-God kind of life as a reality on earth. It begins in the Garden of Eden and crescendos in the incarnation, life, death and resurrection of Jesus and the sending of the Spirit." – Dallas Willard, from *Becoming Dallas Willard: The Formation of a Philosopher, Teacher and Christ Follower*, by Gary Moon

---

Genesis 1:2

Now the earth was formless and empty, darkness was over the surface of the deep and the Spirit of God was hovering over the waters.

Even the most dogmatic proponent of evolution by accident would have a hard time finding fault with the first half of this verse. It's this phrase that doesn't fit the evolutionist view held by many: *"and the Spirit of God was hovering."*

"The Spirit" gives us our first clue that the Trinity existed before creation. Before humans, there was love and relationship within the Trinity. We learn more about the three-fold nature of God when Jesus arrives on the scene.

Love and communication are by design

When God created the first humans in His image, love and a desire to communicate with others (form relationships) became natural and essential aspects of every human personality. For this reason, when someone asks why humans seek love and relationships, we Christians can explain that these desires are placed in us by God's deliberate design. He made love and communication as important to us as they are to the triune nature of His being.

An evolutionist who denies God can only posit theories about how love and communication developed out of inanimate matter. These theories dive into the realm of chemical reactions, usually related to self-survival and natural selection. None of them explain how chemicals and survival instincts can create personality out of an empty, impersonal void.

Rocking the law of natural selection

We certainly do not see the impersonal becoming personal in nature. Rocks, for instance, have not learned over time how to love and communicate. What most theories fail to take into account is that love and concern for human life go well beyond survival needs, even extending to those who are highly unlovable or dangerous.

If survival is the foundation of personality, how do we account for those who are willing to risk their lives to save others? Why are so many unwilling to sanction the death of an unrepentant, still dangerous murderer?

Where does this respect for life come from? And why are humans wired to seek justice for the weak, the sick, the hungry and the oppressed? The laws of natural selection would seem to argue for allowing the weak and violent to die because that is nature's way of keeping the herd strong and safe.

A Christ follower says respect for life exists because we are made in the image of our Creator, who has built into each of us the echoes of His voice. If we can't – or won't – acknowledge our Creator, we have no logical explanation.

What we find in Genesis and throughout Scripture is that there have always been women and men who recognize the one true God, just as there have always been those who make their own gods.

The Old Testament Book of Jeremiah speaks of false gods in Chapter 10:1-16. Those verses tell us that God is not like an idol made of gold or other earthly materials, nor is He a god made from the human imagination.

Like Jeremiah, Moses knew the difference between the living God and false gods. He may have lived a long time ago, he may now seem seriously "old-school," but he was an intelligent, discerning writer and national leader at a critical point in his nation's history and he spoke to God face to face.

God-created distinctions at the beginning of space-time history

In the first two verses of Genesis, we see God at work as He creates a new world that is still without form or life. From verse 3 on, the story unfolds and there is an evolution from unformed matter to something more distinct. Beginning with verses 3-8, Moses points out eight God-created stepping stones in the process that gave form to our world.

Steps one and two

Genesis 1:3-8

And God said, "Let there be light," and there was light. 4 God saw that the light was good and he separated the light from the darkness. 5 God called the light "day," and the darkness he called "night." And there was evening and there was morning—the first day. 6 And God said, "Let there be a vault between the waters to separate water from water." 7 So God made the vault and separated the water under the vault from the water above it. And it was so. 8 God called the vault "sky." And there was evening and there was morning—the second day.

After describing the initial creation of matter, Moses uses the word "separate" (or "divide") over and over in Chapter 1. In almost every case, these distinctive steps are introduced with "let," as we see in the New American Standard Bible (NASB) translation of verses 3-8: *"Let there be light," "Let there be an expanse in the midst of the waters,"* and *"let it separate the waters from the waters."*

Picture a dark, swirling, cloudy mass composed of all the elements needed to finish the job, including water. In effect, God says, "Let it be this way," and something that already exists is

changed from what it was to something different. Creation
is a process.

What scientists say

"Ever since the discovery of organic molecules in a meteorite
that landed in Australia about half a century ago, scientists have
been tantalized by the possibility that the building blocks of life
originated in space. New research is shedding light on how such
compounds might have formed and found their way to Earth,"
Ker Than, *Smithsonian Magazine*, February 2013.

To me, this is an indication that science is catching up with
Scripture, not moving farther away. That Genesis and modern
science line up so well at this point in the creation story is all the
more amazing when we realize Moses did not have a scientific
background or roughly 3,400 years of scientific discoveries to
draw on.

Where most evolutionary scientists differ from Moses is that
they insist the swirling mass became orderly and purposeful
all by itself, with no outside direction or design. Moses, on the
other hand, describes how God begins to organize and shape His
creation, the first step being the separation of darkness and light
(pointed out by Moses in verses 3-5).

One simple way of defining light is that it is "nature's" way of
transferring energy through space. Because energy is essential to
the creation process, it is not surprising that the creation of light
is God's first transformational step.

Firmament in the midst of waters

The second step is found in verse 6 and relates directly to
the quote from *Smithsonian Magazine*. Moses writes about the
creation of an expanse, or firmament, in the midst of the waters.
"Space" is probably the best equivalent to firmament for today's
readers. Firmament has a broad meaning. It can be where the

moons, stars, planets and galaxies are found (verse 14) or the sky, where birds soar above us (verse 20).

Verse 6 indicates that the swirling expanse that became our highly ordered universe contained a massive amount of water. This was confusing until science caught up with Moses thousands of years later. But how did Moses know there was water in the far reaches of space?

Even today, finding water in the heavens is a big deal, as evidenced by an article on the NASA website dated July 22, 2011: "Two teams of astronomers have discovered the largest and farthest reservoir of water ever detected in the universe. The water, equivalent to 140 trillion times all the water in the world's oceans, is more than 112 billion light-years away." According to NASA scientist Matt Bradford, "It's another demonstration that water is pervasive throughout the universe, even at the very earliest times."

Skeptics might reason that it was a lucky guess or that Moses copied a myth that accidentally conforms to reality, but that's because it is easier for them to distrust the accuracy of Moses than to accept that this ancient Jewish writer, a man with no apparent background in science, wrote the truth long before anyone could verify it by scientific methods.

How long is a day?

An important thought to keep in mind while reading Genesis 1-3 is that difficult questions are common when we dig deep into the Bible. The world is complex and God, who exists outside of our world, is even more so. To expect that the infinite God will choose to communicate everything about everything to us finite humans is not reasonable. We who live inside the created world can never assimilate all there is to know about the finite world, let alone the infinite world that God lives in.

One of the vexing questions for many who read this part of Genesis is this: "How long is a day?" The first day mentioned is in verse 5 and it refers to a time before God creates the firmament (space) or the sun, moon, stars and planets. To have a 24-hour day as we think of it, we need the Earth in its orbit around the sun.

The word for "day" used in the Hebrew is "yom," which appears in the Hebrew text of the Old Testament nearly 1,500 times. It is translated as: time, day, today, forever, continually, age and perpetually. In English, it can mean a 24-hour or solar day, a figure of speech covering a considerable time or a number of years.

In Scripture, the context determines how the word is to be translated, but it's not always easy to discern. What, then, can we say about the first chapter of Genesis? Given that verse 5 uses "day" before the elements exist to allow the timing of a solar day, I believe that Moses is speaking of an indeterminate period of time.

In 2 Peter 3:8, the apostle tells us: *"But do not forget this one thing, dear friends: With the Lord a day is like a thousand years and a thousand years are like a day."* The context of Peter's letter is that some were complaining God was late to deliver on his promise to redeem His people. Peter reminds them – and us – that God's time is not the same as our time.

The reality is that time is only relevant to us humans because our days on Earth are limited. Perhaps the best way to deal with this issue is to recognize that the most important historical fact is that God created. How long the creation process took may be of interest, but what's critical is that God was, and still is, fully in control.

Steps three and four

Genesis 1:9-13

And God said, "Let the water under the sky be gathered to one place and let dry ground appear." And it was so. 10 God called the dry ground "land," and the gathered waters he called "seas." And God saw that it was good. 11 Then God said, "Let the land produce vegetation: seed-bearing plants and trees on the land that bear fruit with seed in it, according to their various kinds." And it was so. 12 The land produced vegetation: plants bearing seed according to their kinds and trees bearing fruit with seed in it according to their kinds. And God saw that it was good. 13 And there was evening and there was morning—the third day.

Verse 9 describes the third step, saying: *"let dry ground appear."* God continues to refine our world and now separates out sea and land. In verse 11, we see a fourth distinctive step, one that separates things that are not alive from vegetation that is alive. Not only are the living and non-living noted separately (an important distinction that is at odds with pantheistic beliefs), but God shows Himself to be the master gardener by giving us a variety of plant life right from the start. He brings forth vegetation, plants yielding seed after their kind and trees bearing fruit with seed in them after their kind. I particularly like knowing that God enjoyed His work and *"saw that it was good."*

Step five

Genesis 1:14-19

And God said, "Let there be lights in the vault of the sky to separate the day from the night and let them serve as signs to mark sacred times and days and years,

15 and let them be lights in the vault of the sky to give light on the earth." And it was so. 16 God made two great lights—the greater light to govern the day and the lesser light to govern the night. He also made the stars. 17 God set them in the vault of the sky to give light on the earth, 18 to govern the day and the night and to separate light from darkness. And God saw that it was good. 19 And there was evening and there was morning—the fourth day.

The fifth step is when God makes lights in the vault of the sky (space) and divides Earth's day from night. The creation continues to develop.

The order of creation in Genesis is amazingly accurate scientifically when compared to what scientists know after 3,400 years of study. But that doesn't mean there aren't questions. One of them is right here, where Moses follows the creation of vegetation with God defining the *"two great lights"* (sun and moon). Some students of Genesis wonder how plants can precede the sunlight necessary to grow them.

If you recall, light is introduced in verses 3-5. Now light is being created again here. It appears that light is first introduced to the universe and then fine-tuned for Earth by the introduction of the sun and moon.

In verses 3-5, the Hebrew word for light is "'or," from a root meaning "illumination." In verses 14-19, the word for lights is "maor," from a root meaning "a luminous body." So, first we get light, then come luminous bodies that direct light to the surface of the Earth.

It is entirely possible that during the ordering of the universe God provided enough light to grow plants before the sun was in place. The universe was in a state of flux; we have no way of knowing what conditions existed on the face of the Earth. Because I am just barely too young to have watched the creation process for myself, I have decided to trust that God gave the plants enough light to flourish at the appropriate time. Given His track record for providing what His creation needs when it needs it, my faith seems justified.

Step six

Genesis 1:20-23

And God said, "Let the water teem with living creatures and let birds fly above the earth across the vault of the sky." 21 So God created the great creatures of the sea and every living thing with which the water teems and that moves about in it, according to their kinds and every winged bird according to its kind. And God saw that it was good. 22 God blessed them and said, "Be fruitful and increase in number and fill the water in the seas and let the birds increase on the earth." 23 And there was evening and there was morning—the fifth day.

The sixth step is the creation of conscious life. Up to now, the only life on Earth is vegetation, which we can refer to as "unconscious life" (living but not mindful, aware or sensible). Unlike vegetation, sea life and birds are very much aware of what is going on around them.

In verse 21, Moses' could have used a Hebrew word such as "asah" or "yatsar" for "created" or "formed." Instead, he chose "bara," a word that emphasizes God was creating something entirely new. "Bara" is always used with God as its subject, specifically when referring to His ability to make something new or something out of nothing, as in Genesis 1:1, 1:21, 1:27, Genesis 5:1-2 and Deuteronomy 4:32.

Though Moses tells us that God created various kinds of creatures that never existed before, he does not make it clear if these "kinds" of creatures came into being instantly or over time (unless "yom" is meant to specify a solar day). That leaves the process and time frame open to speculation.

To this point in the Genesis account, science is still on board with the sequence, if not the originator of the sequence.

Step seven

Genesis 1:24-25:

And God said, "Let the land produce living creatures according to their kinds: the livestock, the creatures that move along the ground and the wild animals, each according to its kind." And it was so. 25 God made the wild animals according to their kinds, the livestock according to their kinds and all the creatures that move along the ground according to their kinds. And God saw that it was good.

In this seventh step, God creates conscious life on Earth that is distinguished from conscious life in the water or in the air. He has now created everything except humans. Science is still on board with the sequence.

The NIV Bible translates verse 24 as *"Let the land produce living creatures according to their kinds."* I take this to mean that God planned out their "kinds," but they came into being through a process He set in motion (*"Let the land produce"*).

As with the sea creatures, we don't know what that process looked like because Moses does not tell us. To me, this leaves open the possibility that at least some "living creatures" went through stages of development, as evolutionists claim.

Step eight

Genesis 1:26-28

Then God said, "Let us make mankind in our image, in our likeness, so that they may rule over the fish in the sea and the birds in the sky, over the livestock and all the wild animals, and over all the creatures that move along the ground." 27 So God created mankind in his own image, in the image of God he created them; male and female he created them. 28 God blessed them and said to them, "Be fruitful and increase in number; fill the earth and subdue it. Rule over the fish in the sea and the birds in the sky and over every living creature that moves on the ground."

Now comes trouble in the science lab! The ancient author with the remarkable understanding of the order of creation tells us how we got here: God created us. Not only that, Moses says He created us in His image, thus making humans the eighth step in God's evolutionary process.

There is a lot to consider in this section of Scripture. First, where Moses writes "man," read "human" or "humanity." (I'll explain below.) Second, notice that God said, *"Let us make."* Throughout the Bible, we are told there is only one God and there is no other like him. Yet verse 26 says "us." God is again referring to His triune nature, that of Father, Son and Holy Spirit.

Moses introduced the Holy Spirit in verse 2. There are three distinct aspects to God's being, all united in perfect love and communication. Verses 2 and 26 both indicate that the Trinity existed before our finite world was created. Other such references include Genesis 3:22, Isaiah 6:18, John 1:1-3 and John 1:14-15.

This same God of creation later becomes flesh, stooping down to make Himself known, much as an adult gets down to eye level to talk with a small child. God's willingness to lower Himself to the human level, His desire to maintain a relationship with us, is evidence of the nature of His love (John 17:4-5). I like the way this point is emphasized by *Mary Did You Know,* a song written by Mark Lowry, which includes this line: "[Mary did you know] when you kiss your little baby, you have kissed the face of God?"

Because God is relational and we are made in His image, we know we are designed to be relational. Our inner spirit, or character, is made to be in tune with His. Rocks, trees, fish, birds, animals and the Earth itself are important parts of God's good creation, but none are imbued with His own image.

We have been given a unique place in this world, with responsibilities unique to humans. We are not God – or even little gods – but we exist because of an act of will by a Creator who is both eternal and personal. When we understand who God is we can begin to understand who we are in relation to Him and to one another.

Elaborating on "adam"

Moses writes that God said, *"Let Us make mankind in Our image."* The Hebrew word he uses for mankind is "adam." It means "humanity in general, both male and female." The Hebrew word that indicates a specific man is "ish."

Later in Genesis, the first man is given the name of "Adam." As a proper noun, "Adam" reinforces the connection between Earth and humanity and, I think, gives an insight into God's sense of humor. Where's the humor? The Hebrew word for ground is "adamah." Adam the human is formed from the dust of the "adamah."

Ignore the pun if you will, but be sure to pay attention to the distinction between humanity in general (adam) and the specific man (ish). Many preachers and Bible commentators do not. The meaning of the text is easily distorted if we lose sight of whether these Genesis references are about women and men in general, men only, women only or specific individuals.

It is important to recognize that in verses 26 and 27 Moses again uses "bara" when describing God's creation of the first humans. Even though we learn in Genesis 2 that God formed Adam out of material he had already created and he made Eve out of Adam, they are entirely new creatures.

The most startling distinction between these two humans and other forms of conscious and unconscious life, we're told, is that they carry God's image.

Are men and women to compete for power?

The two humans are God's last major step in the creation process. These special beings have an equally special new role. In verses 26 and 27, God reveals that men and women are both to rule over all the Earth (Rule over it: put it under positive control, guard, guide).

Please notice that nowhere does Moses write that God's plan is for one of his first humans to rule over the other. That could put them in competition for power instead of working together to guide and protect the created world. When power is the goal, "me" frequently ends up stepping on "we."

Sadly, we humans have a history of striving for power and prestige, while largely ignoring that we are designed to love and communicate in unity, as seen in the triune God. But let us not jump ahead to Genesis Chapter 2.

Here is God's plan for women and men

The content of verses 26-28 is so important that Moses repeats it several times. Three times Moses tells us that God created humans – male and female – in His image. Two times he writes that women and men are to serve as protectors over creation.

Verse 28 is the first time we know of that God communicates directly with Adam and Eve. This is God, who exists outside of what He created, speaking to those who are inside of His creation. From the beginning, it is normal for God to speak directly to humans within space-time history. How sad it is that for millions the phrase *"then God said [to them]"* is now a stumbling block. "Can you hear me now?" takes on a whole new meaning in this context. Can you picture God with a smartphone in hand, wondering why the humans He created won't answer His call?

God puts the emphasis on "them"

When verse 28 tells us about God's first message to his first humans, who specifically is He speaking to? Moses says God is talking to "them." We know this because every time he writes "man" in verses 26-28 he chooses the Hebrew word for humanity, "adam," which includes both men and women.

Understanding this, do you see a difference in the roles of men and women or any difference in how God relates to Adam and Eve at this point in Genesis? I hope not; there is no difference. God speaks to both the man and woman. The woman and man are blessed by God. The woman and man are told to be fruitful and multiply. And the woman and man are given the responsibility for ruling over birds, animals and sea creatures. Does this change later? Keep reading.

Genesis 1:29-30

Then God said, "I give you every seed-bearing plant on the face of the whole earth and every tree that has fruit with seed in it. They will be yours for food. 30 And to all the beasts of the earth and all the birds in the sky and all the creatures that move along the ground — everything that has the breath of life in it — I give every green plant for food." And it was so.

Now that Adam and Eve are assigned as caretakers of God's creation, He tells them what He is providing for their food and what is to be eaten by other living creatures.

What, no BBQ for Adam and Eve?

In all the decades I have read and reread Genesis, it took until the writing of this book for me to realize that God gave Adam and Eve a vegetarian diet. (*"I give you every seed-bearing plant on the face of the whole earth and every tree that has fruit with seed in it. They will be yours for food."*)

I also noticed that even animals which now eat each other, and some which eat humans, did not originally eat meat. (*"And to all the beasts of the earth and all the birds in the sky and all the creatures that move along the ground — everything that has the breath of life in it — I give every green plant for food."*)

It is interesting that God provides two distinct types of food, one for humans and one for animals. This further emphasizes the difference between humans and animals. Verses 29 and 30 also show us that God never intended for humans or animals to compete for food.

From the outset of humanity, God provided food that was appropriate for both; they didn't want, or need, to eat one another. I'm not trying to construct a theology for vegetarianism, only reporting what is in the first three chapters of Genesis. See the discussion of Chapter 3 for new information about who can eat what after the Fall.

Genesis 1:31

God saw all that he had made and it was very good. And there was evening and there was morning — the sixth day.

After a busy six days (solar days or otherwise), God steps back and looks at His creation. He likes what He sees. He likes the way the universe is formed. He likes the way the stars and planets look and how they affect one another. He likes the beauty of the Earth. He likes the sea life and animal and bird life He created. And He likes the humans so much He feels good about giving them responsibility over the rest of His marvelous creation.

If God has a soft, comfy reclining lounge chair in heaven, He must have tilted it back at the end of day six, put up his feet and relaxed, knowing that His newly created universe was humming like a perfectly conceived and magnificently executed work of kinetic art. He also knew, of course, that there would be pain in this birth process, but for the moment, all was exactly as He wanted it.

Genesis 1 — Main points summarized

1. Genesis is a historical account of the beginning of space-time history. The only way I can read it as anything less is to believe that Jesus and his apostles taught fiction or the New Testament references to the Old Testament never happened. In either case, that would make the Bible as trustworthy as a politician's campaign promises and we may as well learn about our Creator from stories about Harry Potter or Spider-Man.

2. God is the creator of the heavens, Earth, seas and all living things. We don't live in an accidental and meaningless universe.

3. God exists in an infinite spirit world that is outside of our human universe, though He can and does enter His created world at times of His choosing.

4. God created humans and put us on Earth for a purpose. That purpose is to be in relationship with Him and with one another. He also charges us with watching over His creation as caretakers, not as ruthless exploiters.

5. The triune (three-person) nature of God has always existed. Thus, relationship is an essential element of God's character and of ours. We know this because God chose to create us in His image.

6. Women and men are given responsibility for taking care of God's creation. There is nothing in Chapter 1 to indicate that God desires Adam to have authority over Eve or vice versa.

Genesis Chapter 2

Key thought:

God planned out and created a real place, the Garden of Eden, for two real humans, Adam and Eve.

Genesis 2:1-3 (NASB translation)

Thus the heavens and the earth were completed and all their hosts. 2 By the seventh day God completed His work which he had done and He rested on the seventh day from all His work which He had done. 3 Then God blessed the seventh day and sanctified it, because in it He rested from all His work which God had created and made.

The ancient Hebrew and Greek Bible texts were not broken into chapters and verses. That was done much later, to make reading and studying the Bible more convenient. Sometimes, as in this case, the chapter breaks are a bit of a puzzle. Here, the first three verses of Chapter 2 really should be the last three of Chapter 1.

The seventh-day rest

By the seventh day, God has completed His work of creation and He takes a rest. Once again, the use of "day" in verse 2 (yom) leaves the meaning open to solar day or an unspecified period of time.

It is significant that God *"blessed the seventh day and sanctified it."* To "bless" a day means to set it apart, to show favor or benefit. To sanctify is to dedicate, purify or make holy. God is speaking something good into being for the benefit of men and women. There is a rhythm to God's life, just as He intends for us. Ideally, we have times of work separated by times of rest. We do well when we can stop regularly to rest, worship, listen, encourage and be encouraged.

Rest is not just to refresh our bodies, but to refresh our spirits as well, through spending time with our Heavenly Father, our family and friends. God is relational and has designed us to be the same.

Is Moses telling us that the Sabbath should be kept as a holy day or is he introducing a rhythm for living that involves work, rest, worship and relationship? I lean toward the latter. It appears that God is introducing an important principle at this point in history but not issuing a law of the Sabbath to His first humans. Later, Israel will institutionalize the keeping of the Sabbath by God's command (Exodus 23:12).

A few months after I drafted these paragraphs, a Sunday sermon by our pastor, Jake Hendrix, added an insight I'd missed. He pointed out that on the seventh day, a day of rest, God still chose to create something. He sanctified these times of rest; He made them holy.

In our culture, time spent at rest is not often seen as spiritually holy. The more common view is that time has value as a resource and it shouldn't be wasted, as illustrated by the phrase, "Time is money." Ben Franklin made that saying popular in 1748, but the same thought can be found all the way back in ancient Greece (circa 430 B.C.) when Antiphon wrote, "The most costly outlay is time."

Even though God demonstrated the importance of rest at the beginning of creation, there is a huge gap in human history where there is no record of any culture on Earth following His rhythm of work, rest, work.

It wasn't until the Jews were rescued from 400 years of slavery in Egypt – where they got no rest ever – that God said, in effect: "You are my people and I want you to take a break every seventh day like I did. And even the land will get a break every seven years." Deuteronomy gives the details.

In Deuteronomy 12:9 and in 21 other Old Testament verses, the Hebrew word "menuchah" (men-oo-kaw) is used for rest, quiet, still, place of comfort and peace. Because this God-instituted day of rest also became a metaphor for eternal rest, the word "menuchah" is used as a synonym for eternal life.

As a result of their practice of resting every seventh day, the Jews were mocked by those around them. An example comes from Seneca, a Roman philosopher who lived during the time of Jesus. Seneca famously said that observing the Sabbath, as the Jewish day of rest was known, wasted one-seventh of their lives. Seneca's sharp mind lacked the wisdom to understand that regular times of rest give us access to the inner rhythm of creation itself; therefore, as Jake noted, it is wise to take our cues from God, rather than our culture.

Rebellion and rest don't mix

At the time of Jake's sermon, I was doing a personal study of Hebrews and was struck by the rest-related warning against ignoring God found in Chapters 3 and 4. The background for the story is that God selected Moses to lead somewhere between 500,000 and 4 million descendants of Abraham out of Egypt. With God going before the Jews to protect and guide them, they were heading for their promised place of physical and spiritual rest, which was only about 240 miles away. That was a month's march.

Despite God's presence and His promise to keep them safe, the people almost immediately began to complain and rebel against Him. Though God warned and disciplined them, they continued to rebel. Eventually, God's patience wore out and His anger burned against them. The result was this declaration: *"In my anger, they shall never enter my rest"* (Hebrews 3:11).

In short order, they went from serving cruel Egyptian slave lords to a rescued nation under God's protection and then to an ungrateful and rebellious people. Because they did not trust God, He caused them to wander in the desert for 40 years, until the adults who left Egypt with Moses were dead. Only two faithful men, Joshua and Caleb, were allowed to enter the Promised Land.

Encourage one another as long as it is today

The author of Hebrews points back in time to this example of rebellion and implores his readers not to die within easy reach of their promised rest. (He's writing to people who have already pledged to follow Jesus, but who apparently are wavering.) He writes: *"Encourage one another daily, as long as it is called 'Today,' so that none of you may be hardened by sin's deceitfulness. We have come to share in Christ, if indeed we hold our original conviction firmly to the very end"* (Hebrews 3:13-14).

Today, as then, the choice to follow our Creator or turn away from Him has serious immediate and long-term implications. We see that in the lives of Adam and Eve. They didn't listen to God and were forced to leave a perfect paradise of relationship, rest and serenity to enter a world that was neither peaceful nor at rest. Like the rescued Jewish slaves who refused to listen to God, Adam and Eve died within easy reach of their place of rest and serenity.

The Book of Hebrews reinforces many similar Bible lessons about trusting and resting in God. The good news pronounced by the author of Hebrews is that as long as it is *"today"* it is not too late to take a firmer grip on our *"original conviction"* or to reach out to God for the first time. The implied warning, however, is that at some point it will no longer be *"today,"* and then it will be too late.

Those who refuse to listen to the voice of God often say they can't possibly believe in a Creator who would condemn anyone to eternal anguish. What these verses from Hebrews make clear is that it is each individual's choice to spend life in God's loving presence or to reject His offer of rest and spend eternity in a space where rest and love do not exist.

If you're reading this, it is still today. If you haven't already done so, now is the time to listen to your Creator. Now is the time to choose God and enjoy His rest.

All their hosts

The phrase *"all their hosts"* deserves some attention before we move on. It denotes the totality of beings that fill the heavens and Earth, as seen in Nehemiah 9:6. Thus, Genesis 2:1 is telling us that God has completed His entire creation. I take this to mean that He has now set in motion all that He plans to set in motion, not that the universe or the living organisms within it will never change from here on out. In other Scriptures, the word "host" is used in a plural form to refer to moon, sun and stars. An example is found in Deuteronomy 17:3. The phrase *"heavenly hosts"* and similar phrases also apply to the angels, in 1Kings 22:19, Isaiah 24:21, Nehemiah 9:6, Psalm 148:2.

Genesis 2:4

This is the account of the heavens and the earth when they were created, when the Lord God made the earth and the heavens.

A more direct translation of the first part of this verse is: *"These are the generations of the heavens and the earth."* The word "generations" is a translation of the Hebrew word "toledoth" (pronounced to-led-aw), a term that is used to separate the Book of Genesis into sections. Each "toledoth" statement ends a historical account.

In this case, the following text – from verse 2:5 through verse 5:2 (where we find the next "toledoth" statement) – contains a new account in the history of creation. Moses now begins to focus on the Garden of Eden, the creation of Adam and Eve and the role of humans as caretakers of the Earth and mates for one another.

From this point on Moses is not looking backward to repeat what he has already told us in Chapter 1; he is looking forward to what comes next. This view is consistent with the way the "toledoth" statements are used in the rest of Genesis and it is important to remember this when faced with the Chapter 2 statements that seem, at first reading, to contradict Chapter 1.

Some scholars believe the first half of verse 4 puts an end bracket on Chapter 1, while the second half of verse 4 is the real beginning of Chapter 2. This is because the first half talks about the heavens and the Earth, while the second part of the verse switches it to the Earth and the heavens. At any rate, with this verse we are now moving into a new part of the creation story.

The word for day used in this verse is "yom," as previously, but in this case we can see clearly that it means "age or season," not a specific period of time. Notice that Moses does not write: "This is an allegory about life on Earth." His claim is that he is writing a historical account of the process by which God created the heavens and the Earth. In our present culture, being asked to believe in the reality of the Garden causes belief issues for many Christians and hysteria among those who, by faith, have ruled out the possibility of God as Creator. The latter view, of course, also rules out the possibility of supernatural events caused by God.

Is science totally objective?

Resistance to God often comes from the scientifically minded, who think they can separate personal beliefs from factual data. But just how objective are they when claiming they reject only what can't be proven by science?

Richard Dawkins, scientist and author of *The God Delusion*, is one of the most vocal spokesmen for that part of the scientific community which rejects the possibility of a Creator. Dawkins is a proponent of what I refer to as the religion of science ("religion" being a set of beliefs concerning the cause, nature and purpose of the universe). His faith causes him to reject eyewitness accounts of historical events, not because he knows they aren't true, but because he is certain – by faith – they can't be.

But Dawkins is far from alone in allowing his personal belief system to overrule facts or rational arguments. It is a myth that scientists uniformly set aside normal human biases and preconceptions when analyzing scientific data and drawing conclusions about the nature of our universe.

Science is based on an accumulation of theories and data collected and tested over time. These form scientific tradition which is the basis of what we consider to be current scientific truth. No human is completely neutral when evaluating concepts or hard data.

We all carry with us personal viewpoints formed from the beginnings of our lives and shaped right up to the present. We have been educated by humans who filter the information they teach through their own personal viewpoints and belief systems. We have personal experiences, wants and desires that influence how we evaluate information. And we all make mistakes.

While objectivity may be the goal of science, it is a human reality that every scientist carries personal viewpoints to work each day. Those who have already ruled out what is and isn't possible about God can't help but develop scientific traditions and "facts" that are a mix of the objective and subjective. Thus, personal bias is always going to be involved in determining scientific "fact."

A scientist who rejects God may insist that we who believe in Him only see God in creation because we are looking for Him. But the converse is also true. A person who does not believe in God or the supernatural focuses on looking for impersonal causes.

"Science is not a catalogue of known facts; it is the discovery of new forms of ignorance. ... *I do wish people would teach children this about science: that it is the richest source of new mysteries. ... About the only safe conclusion about human prehistory — as revealed in genes, stone tools and bones — is that some gigantic new surprises are in store for us. And that is the beauty of science: the more you find out, the more you realise what you did not know."* — From the blog of Matt Ridley, award-winning science writer. (See: http://www.mattridley.co.uk/blog/science-discovers-new-ignorance-about-the-past.aspx)

Science is an ongoing process of discovery

As Matt Ridley points out, scientific truth is a moving target. No matter how much we learn about our universe, it is not likely that scientists will ever discover all there is to know about it. Given that we don't know it all and that the fact of today may at any moment become yesterday's mistaken theory, it would seem that Dawkins and others like him would be wise not to look down on those who hold differing views of the world.

Impartiality takes a hit

There is yet another factor that affects how a scientist can be so right in his or her field of study and so wrong in other areas. As Lesslie Newbigin explains in his book, *The Gospel in a Pluralist Society,* it is possible to understand the mechanics of a language without understanding the meanings within the traditions of that language.

In other words, Dawkins and other scientists who reject God as Creator live inside and understand the traditions of their scientific studies, but they read the Bible as outsiders who do not understand the developed truths and data of Christianity. They're like people who have read about cars but have never driven them. They won't fully understand until they get behind the wheel.

Dawkins' own words tell us how impartial he is in his search for truth: "The Bible should be taught, but emphatically not as reality. It is fiction, myth, poetry, anything but reality." Dawkins claims, "Religion is capable of driving people to such dangerous folly that faith seems to me to qualify as a kind of mental illness."

Dawkins defines a delusion as "something that people believe in despite a total lack of evidence." He undergirds that statement with: "Faith is belief in spite of, even perhaps because of, the lack of evidence." Ironically – failing to see his own inconsistency – he then writes, "We cannot, of course, disprove God, just as we can't disprove Thor, fairies, leprechauns and the Flying Spaghetti Monster."

If Dawkins "cannot, of course, disprove God," then his mocking of those who believe in God is based on faith, not science. Thus, by his own words, Dawkins' colorful hyperbole convicts him as one who is suffering from "a kind of mental illness." In my youth, this was called making a monkey of oneself.

Keeping it real – but congenial

My reason for using Dawkins as an example is to illustrate a contemporary mindset that is making it almost impossible to have a friendly, rational exchange of ideas about the supernatural these days. We need to get past this sort of uncivil behavior or our world will only continue to degenerate into ugly divisions.

A sign of true wisdom and maturity, I believe, is when a person is able to listen to the thoughts of someone else carefully, consider them thoroughly and respond respectfully. We can learn from one another by testing our beliefs against each other. But we can't learn from others, change opinions or make new friends by shutting them out or exchanging insults. That only widens the divide between us.

Defining "Lord God" (Jehovah Elohim)

The phrase *"Lord God"* is used for the first time in Genesis 2:4. The Hebrew words are "Jehovah Elohim." In Genesis 1 we read that: "God said," "God made," and "God created." The Hebrew word used for God in each of these references is "Elohim." The most common use of Elohim is as a personal name for God or when referring to Him as the true God among false gods.

The *New Unger's Bible Dictionary* adds that "Elohim (God) is used when Gentiles speak or are spoken to, or spoken about, unless there is a specific reference to Jehovah, the God of the chosen people. Elohim is used when God is contrasted with men or things, or when the sense requires a common rather than a proper noun."

Jehovah is the proper name of God. Jehovah means "self-existent" or "eternal." Jehovah is also the name that indicates God's special relationship as savior and redeemer to His chosen people. A good way to translate Jehovah Elohim is "the eternal (or self-existent) supreme God." Jehovah is found in Scripture as the consonants YHWH, which are also written as Yahweh, Yehovah or Lord. The letters YHWH form a word, or words, that most scholars translate as "I AM who I AM," "I will be who I will be," or "the Self-Existent One."

In Exodus 3:13-14 Moses says to God, *"Suppose I go to the Israelites and say to them, 'The God of your fathers has sent me to you,' and they ask me, 'What is his name?' Then what shall I tell them?" God said to Moses, "I AM WHO I AM. This is what you are to say to the Israelites: 'I AM has sent me to you.'"* Another account of God making himself known to Moses is found in Exodus 34:6-7. In verse 6, the NIV translation says God refers to himself as, *"The Lord, the Lord."* The same verse in the King James Version (KJV) is translated this way: *"The Lord, The Lord God, merciful and gracious, long suffering and abundant in goodness and truth, Keeping mercy for thousands, forgiving iniquity and transgression and sin and that will by no means clear the guilty."*

Genesis Chapter 3 uses "Lord God" throughout the narrative of the Fall and connects this name with the idea of salvation. If Lord (Jehovah) indicates God's special relationship with the Jews and Elohim is used more generically to include Gentiles, could "Jehovah Elohim," as used here in Chapter 2, already be giving us a hint about the future, when God's people will be those who choose to be His – both Jews and Gentiles?

Genesis 2:5-7

Now no shrub had yet appeared on the earth and no plant had yet sprung up, for the LORD God had not sent rain on the earth and there was no one to work the ground, 6 but streams came up from the earth and watered the whole surface of the ground. 7 Then the

LORD God formed a man from the dust of the ground and breathed into his nostrils the breath of life and the man became a living being.

These verses appear to tell us that plants are not yet growing on the Earth when man arrives, but in Chapter 1 plants come before humans. Responses to this and other questions of sequence cause some to throw up their arms and throw out their Bibles in the same motion. Others resort to philosophical arguments about the meanings of words and the intent of the author.

The first thing I do is remind myself that God would only select authors for the Bible who are intelligent, accurate and honest. The second is to realize how good God is at His job. He employed numerous independent authors over a roughly 1,500-year period to produce the Bible. Despite all the authors and all the translations, God's book exhibits remarkable continuity and cohesiveness from cover to cover.

In short, He has proven Himself a far better editor and publisher than any human could ever hope to be. So if God knows what He's doing and Moses is a talented author, what's the story with these apparent conflicts?

Coming to grips with the question

Let's look more carefully at verses 5-7. For starters, remember that the "toledoth" statement in verse 4 indicates that what follows is looking forward, not backward.

Next, keep in mind that Chapter 1 provides an overview of the creation process on a global scale and Chapter 2 zooms in on a particular part of the Earth to give us a more personal look at God and the first humans. The emphasis at this point in Genesis 2 is not on a creation sequence; it's on what is happening between God and humans.

I see two ways to read Genesis 2:5-7. Either Moses is reminding us that God prepared the plants that grow on Earth or he is writing more specifically about how God is preparing the Garden of Eden for Adam and Eve.

The new information presented here is that plant-life appeared as part of a process. All plant life did not just appear fully grown. The NASB translation of Genesis 2:5 implies that the vegetation in question existed before being planted (vegetation *"had yet sprouted"*). The KJV translates verse 5 more definitively. It says God made *"every plant of the field before it was in the earth and every herb of the field before it grew."*

The mention in verse 5 that there was not yet anyone to cultivate the ground is significant because it tells us that plants were created before humans, which agrees with the sequence in the first chapter. Verses 5 and 6 also tell us that God determined when to send the first rains.

The point, it seems to me, is that God created a wide variety of plants right from the start, but He didn't cause them to grow until the Earth was ready for them. The order and beauty of the world are planned. They are not accidental. They are the work of a botanist and master gardener of the highest order.

Verse 7 focuses on day six of creation to tell us that God formed a human from the ground – from particles of Earth – and breathed life into him. What happened on days one through five is not important to this part of the story because Moses is concentrating on the humans.

The Lord God formed a human

The Hebrew word for "formed" is "yatsar," meaning to form as a potter shapes clay. Did God literally shape the first man as though He was working with clay or is this figurative? It is probably the latter, but there is not enough information to know for sure.

How God created the first human is a matter of curiosity; the relevant information is that God is our creator.

It is important to see that God makes a distinction between non-human life and human life. When forming plant life, fish, birds and animals, God says "let there be" and it happens. When God creates the first human the words are very personal. We're told that once God forms man He breathes life into him. This is a beautiful picture of the Heavenly Potter giving the finishing touch to His unique new creation.

"This was the scientific age [Referring to when 'On the Origin of Species' was published] and people wanted to believe that their traditions were in line with the new era, but this was impossible if you thought that these myths should be understood literally ... Creation stories had never been regarded as historically accurate; their purpose was therapeutic. But once you start reading Genesis as scientifically valid, you have bad science and bad religion."– A Short History of Myth, by Karen Armstrong, British author and commentator known for her books on comparative religion.

Humans created from dirt? Are you kidding, myth-ter?

More than 3,000 years ago, Moses wrote that God formed man from the dust of the ground. This is one of the Bible "myths" casually dismissed by Karen Armstrong and others.

The Hebrew word translated in Scripture as "dust" is "aphar," which means loose dirt, ground, soil or clay. In 2013, biological engineers from Cornell University's department of Nanoscale Science in New York were excited to report that clay – which at its most basic is a combination of minerals in the ground – acts as a breeding laboratory for tiny molecules and chemicals which it "absorbs like a sponge."

Reporting on the Cornell findings in the journal *Scientific Reports*, researchers said the process takes billions of years, during which the chemicals react to each other to form proteins, DNA and, eventually, living cells. As a result, they believe clay "might have been the birthplace of life on Earth." (http://www.news.cornell.edu/stories/2013/11/chemicals-life-may-have-combined-clay)

Did Adam come into this world as an adult or a metaphor?

Reports from science labs such as the one at Cornell continue to insist that life was created by impersonal accidents and evolved slowly over billions of years, without God's intervention.

Those of us who have found through experience that the Bible is a trustworthy source of history and wisdom insist, as it does, that God created our world and all of its inhabitants. According to Moses, the first humans had the intelligence to converse with God, take care of our world and make life altering choices. Nothing in Genesis suggests to me that he is writing about a metaphorical Adam and Eve or using a creation myth to teach ignorant men and women about life.

Does Moses say they were fully-formed adults from the first moment of their creation or does he leave room for a long, involved process? How each of us interprets "yom" is a key to answering that question.

To an eternal God who lives outside of our space-time boundaries, however, "billions of years" is a reference that doesn't really apply. God could easily have created life in a heartbeat or slowly (according to our measure of time). What we know for sure is He created!

More important than the length of time the process took, I believe, is Cornell University's announcement that "clay might have been the birthplace of life on Earth." This is one more piece of evidence that science is finally catching up with Moses 3,400 years after he wrote Genesis.

Jesus and Paul confirm the reality of Adam and Eve

Surprisingly, even many Christians are not aware that Jesus spoke of Adam and Eve as real figures in history, as discussed earlier in this book (Matthew 19 and Mark 10 give two examples). Likewise, the Apostle Paul writes: *"For it was Adam who was first created and then Eve. And it was not Adam who was deceived, but the woman being deceived, fell into transgression"* (1 Timothy 2:13-14 – NASB. Also see Acts 17).

Paul weighs in again in Romans 5:12-14: *"Therefore, just as through one man sin entered into the world and death through sin and so death spread to all men, because all sinned – for until the Law sin was in the world, but sin is not imputed when there is no law. Nevertheless, death reigned from Adam until Moses, even over those who had not sinned in the likeness of the offense of Adam, who is a type of Him who was to come"* (NASB).

Because the Greek word Paul uses for "man" is "anthrópos," which means a human being or individual man, verse 12 can be read this way: *"Therefore, just as through one human sin entered into the world and so death spread to all humans."*

Yet another example that verifies Adam and Eve were real people is Romans 5:15, which links the historicity of Adam and Jesus with all following generations who accept the grace of God through Jesus. A similar parallelism is repeated in 1 Corinthians 15:21-22: *"For since death came through a man, the resurrection of the dead comes also through a man. For as in Adam all die, so in Christ all will be made alive."* We see the same thought in 1 Corinthians 15:45: *"So it is written: 'The first man Adam, became a living being;*

the last Adam, a life-giving spirit." The *"so it is written"* alludes to Genesis 2:7.

Luke 3:23-38 offers the same type of parallelism when he traces the genealogy of Jesus back through Adam and then to God. These examples link Adam and Eve to a whole group of people we know to have been living humans.

In his book about Genesis, Schaeffer writes, "If we take away the historicity of Adam, we are left with nothing but air. If we mess with this ordinary way of understanding what is written in the Bible, the structure of Christianity is reduced to only an existential leap." And that is exactly what is happening thanks to skeptics such those who participated in the well-known "Jesus Seminar."

The participants of that group decided, in their own modern wisdom, to rewrite or reject the claims of the ancient Bible authors and historians, even though many of them left us with their personal, eyewitness accounts of supernatural events – accounts they were willing to give up their lives to defend. (The Jesus Seminar was composed of scholars and laymen brought together in 1985 by Robert Funk, a self-professed atheist. They went through the New Testament and decided what they thought Jesus really said and did, regardless of what the Bible's authors claimed to have seen with their own eyes and heard with their own ears. Many now take this group's work as truth.)

Adam in the Garden of Eden– A parenthetical thought

Genesis says that the man was the first human created in God's image. What if each of God's days took thousands of years and what if during those thousands of years God created primitive beings that looked human-like, but lacked the one key ingredient that differentiated them from Adam and Eve? That ingredient being "in His image."

What if these primitive beings were a form of conscious life that had an ability to learn, that banded together for survival, and that walked upright on the land? What if these earlier, primitive beings were almost there, except for the inner spark from God that they needed to represent Him here on earth?

When God created Adam and Eve He gave them the same spiritual character He possesses, including a love for others, appreciation of beauty, strong sense of justice and desire for relationship. It appears from Genesis that right from their point of creation Adam and Eve were fully-formed adult humans, able to think, talk, interact with one another, and to do the work God prepared in advance for them. They even entered life with a fully-formed moral sense, able to distinguish right from wrong.

What if, just as the man was incomplete before the woman existed, human beings were incomplete before God breathed His likeness into Adam and Eve?

And finally, what if these pre-Adam and Eve beings died out either before or during the Great Flood, when only Noah and his family were saved? The former could be true; the latter most definitely would have happened. Are flood skeptics missing the boat? Some claim that science has ruled out the Great Flood. Dr. Andrew Snelling, who holds a PhD in Geology, is one of many scientists who uses science to prove the efficacy of the Flood. Dr. Snelling has published dozens of articles on the subject, and his work is easily found on the web. One essay I thought especially interesting is titled, "Geologic Evidences for the Genesis Flood."

As noted earlier, we are not given exhaustive knowledge

of how God has worked within His universe. What God provides for us is what we need to know to be in relationship with Him and with one another. That being the case, we may very well find out what those who've gone before us already know…that the full creation story has twists, turns, and surprises waiting for all of us. How important is it to be right on the "what we think" part? The truth God gives us is more than enough to bring us into relationship with Him, if we are willing.

(I'm aware of theistic evolution theories. My suggestion is different in that I believe Adam and Eve did not evolve; they were created as fully-formed human adults, who could communicate with God and one another, and who knew right from wrong.)

Genesis 2:8-14

Now the Lord God had planted a garden in the east, in Eden; and there he put the man he had formed. 9 The Lord God made all kinds of trees grow out of the ground—trees that were pleasing to the eye and good for food. In the middle of the garden were the tree of life and the tree of the knowledge of good and evil. 10 A river watering the garden flowed from Eden; from there it was separated into four headwaters. 11 The name of the first is the Pishon; it winds through the entire land of Havilah, where there is gold. 12 (The gold of that land is good; aromatic resin and onyx are also there.) 13 The name of the second river is the Gihon; it winds through the entire land of Cush. 14 The name of the third river is the Tigris; it runs along the east side of Ashur. And the fourth river is the Euphrates.

Verses 8-14 can be a stumbling block for those who fail to realize that Moses is now writing about the Garden of Eden. God creates plant life, human life and then the garden. He puts the human in the garden. When verse 8 mentions the man and verse 9 talks about the planting of trees some readers become confused, thinking the sequence is not the same as in Chapter 1.

Keep in mind that Chapter 1 is a global overview of creation and this portion of Chapter 2 is specific to the creation of the garden. There is no conflict with Chapter 1. So far so good. But is the garden a metaphor about life in an eternal paradise or is Moses writing about space-time history? That question just won't go away, will it?

I believe the Garden of Eden is both real and symbolic. Anyone who sees the garden only as a metaphor has to explain why Moses goes to great pains to set the garden's location and describe the plants. That isn't done in metaphors now, nor was it done in ancient times. The obvious conclusion is that Moses is describing a real place, with real vegetation, inhabited by a real man. When we read further in the Bible, it becomes clear that the garden also gives us a foreshadowing of eternity in the presence of God.

There is a problem, however, when we try to locate the garden on a map. Many believe it was in the Mesopotamian region (in or near present-day Iraq). This fits the mention of the Tigris and Euphrates rivers. But it is likely that these rivers were rerouted when the Great Flood covered the Earth in the time of Noah. It is reasonable to expect that such a flood would wipe out all traces of the garden.

Those who argue that the Great Flood is only a metaphor run into the same problem as with the Garden of Eden; both are described in detail, which ancient authors only did when writing of actual events and places. As a consequence, we're left with a choice: Did Moses invent a new form of storytelling or is he writing about real locations and real events in human history?

Because I believe that Moses is writing about the history of Israel, as the rest of his words seem to bear out, I see the Garden of Eden as a quiet, beautiful environment, specially prepared for the humans who would live there. Nothing was lacking to make this an ideal home. It is not a stretch, then, to conclude that the common human desire to create quiet, beautiful living spaces for ourselves – complete with plants, pets, water features and boundaries – points back to the first chapters of Genesis. We're trying to replace what Adam and Eve lost.

Genesis 2:15-17

The Lord God took the man and put him in the Garden of Eden to work it and take care of it. 16 And the Lord God commanded the man, "You are free to eat from any tree in the garden; 17 but you must not eat from the tree of the knowledge of good and evil, for when you eat from it you will certainly die."

Verse 15 tells us for the second time in the chapter that God put *"the man"* (still an unnamed human) in the garden. The difference, this time, is that we learn he was put there to *"work it and take care of it."* From the start, God intends humans to be active, as He is active. Because this garden paradise is beautiful, provides exercise and produces his food, it feeds both the man's body and his spirit.

Once man is in the garden, God tells him which trees are good for food and which he needs to stay away from. Here is the prologue for the soon-to-come collision between human will and the will of our Creator. God's command comes with only one prohibition: *"You are free to eat from any tree in the garden; but you must not eat from the tree of the knowledge of good and evil."*

Only the fruit from one tree is withheld by God and it is not something the man needs in this idyllic setting. God is already providing everything he requires. Well, almost. His wife has not yet come into the picture.

Morality is born

I think it fair to say that what God tells the man in verse 17 provides the first lesson in morality. God's words call the man's attention to both his free will and his responsibilities, as well as introducing him to the idea of consequences.

Man is told that if he eats of the tree of the knowledge of good and evil he will *"certainly die."* We can learn what type of death God means from the kind of life the man loses. It is not physical death on the day he eats the fruit; it is a death that involves loss of innocence; death to his close relationship with God; death to his perfect relationship with the Earth and the other living beings on it; eventual death to his finite body; and, ultimately, the possibility of eternal death (An eternity spent apart from God, who is the source of all love and beauty).

These verses indicate God's absolute right to rule over humans and creation. And they indicate that God created humans with the ability to distinguish right from wrong, as defined by God, not by those of us He created.

Genesis 2:18-20 (NASB translation)

Then the LORD God said, "It is not good for the man to be alone; I will make him a helper suitable for him." 19 Out of the ground the LORD God formed every beast of the field and every bird of the sky and brought them to the man to see what he would call them; and whatever the man called a living creature, that was its name. 20 The man gave names to all the cattle and to the birds

of the sky and to every beast of the field, but for Adam there was not found a helper suitable for him.

Verse 20 is the first time that "adam" is used as a proper noun. Now the man has a name: Adam. By naming him, God once again makes it clear that He has authority over Adam. Because Adam has been given authority over the birds and animals, God allows Adam to name each of them.

Readers trip over verses 18 and 19 for very different reasons. First, there is a great deal of disagreement over God's intention when He says He will make a *"helper suitable"* for Adam. We'll get to that in a moment.

The second stumble is because some believe verse 19 conflicts with the Chapter 1 creation sequence, which tells us that all the living creatures were created on the third day and Adam on the sixth. Here it appears, at first glance, that Adam is formed before the birds and animals. Is this a conflict or is it a misunderstanding? I believe it is the latter.

One explanation is that in Hebrew storytelling, chronological sequence is often less important than the main thread of a story. A better explanation in this case, I believe, has to do with how we translate the Hebrew word for "formed," which is "yatsar." The word can mean "formed," "having formed," or "had formed." Some Bible translations, the NASB being one, use the former. The NIV and others use the latter, which reads: *"Out of the ground the Lord God **had formed** every beast of the field"* (Emphasis added).

The latter translation refers to what God had already done on day three and removes the chronological issue. This means that the plants (Genesis 2:9) and animals (Genesis 2:19) had already been formed by God earlier in the creation sequence. Such an explanation is seen by some modern Bible scholars as changing the text to suit the reader's purpose. I find their skepticism interesting in view of the fact that ancient Jewish scholars, who knew their own language and cultures at least as well as modern scholars, found no conflict in verse 19. Nor did William Tyndale, who in the early 16th century was the first person to translate a Bible into English directly from the Hebrew and Greek texts.

Tyndale translated "yatsar" as "had formed," just as we find in the modern NIV translation: *"And after that the LORD God* **had made** *of the earth all manner beasts of the field and all manner fowls of the air, he brought them unto Adam to see what he would call them. And as Adam called all manner living beasts: even so are their names."* (Tyndale, Genesis 2:19 – emphasis added).

In my view, this paragraph isn't about the order of creation; it's about Adam and Eve. Moses is reminding readers that God formed a man and He formed animal life, but because they are so different, one is not a companion for the other – at least not in the same way that one human is a companion to another.

What the first man needs is someone to talk to, interact with, work beside and be his mate. This verse points to Adam's need for a human relationship. Eve isn't alive yet and, just as the infinite God has fellowship within the spiritual realm of the Trinity, the man needs human companionship within his finite world.

When God brings the birds and animals to Adam and has him name them, He is allowing Adam to discover for himself that birds and animals can keep him company, but none will ever be the best companion for him. That person is about to be introduced as his "helper," and the word will create a controversy that rages to this day.

What does it mean to be man's helper?

The KJV translates the second half of verse 18 as *"I will make him an help meet."* The NIV and NASB translations say *"a helper suitable."* The Hebrew text uses two words for this phrase:

"*ezer kenegdo.*" These are two of the most important words in these first three chapters because they are used to define God's purpose in creating woman.

"'Ezer" means "help" or "helper." The root of the word is "azar," which indicates what type of helper is being created. This root word means to surround, protect, or aid. Nothing in the meaning indicates subservience. "Kenegdo" comes from the root word "neged," which *Strong's Hebrew Dictionary* defines as an opposite, a counterpart or mate, over against.

The sense of "'ezer kenegdo," then, is "an equal but opposite helper to him." Man's helper, according to Moses, does not stand three steps behind man; she stands at his side or facing him. Perhaps it is not a coincidence that Eve was made from a rib that came from Adam's side.

A good way to illustrate this term is to say that a left hand is the "'ezer kenegdo" to a right hand; both hands are equal and look the same, except they are opposites. Their purpose is to work together. We can also say that the "'ezer kenegdo" of the left wing of an airplane is the right wing. They look the same except they are opposite each other; equal but opposite. One wing is no more important than the other. The same is true with man and woman. Man's "'ezer kenegdo" is woman. Both are equal but opposite. This strongly implies that woman's "'ezer kenegdo" is man.

"'Ezer" is used in the Old Testament to describe God as a helper of the Jews (Psalm 33:20, 70:5, 115:9-11, 121:2). In other ancient writings, "'ezer" is used to describe a powerful army that comes to the aid of a lesser army. Because the same Hebrew word that depicts God as Israel's helper also describes Eve as Adam's helper, we know the type of helping described in Genesis is not a matter of someone without power assisting someone who has power.

"Helper" is not a subservient role. The Bible offers numerous examples of God – the source of all power – helping His people when they are powerless. God helps because He loves us, not because He has an obligation to serve us.

We've already seen in Chapter 1 that this "helper" for man is created in the image of God, same as man, and is given responsibility for taking care of the Earth, same as man. At this point in Scripture, there is absolutely no reason to believe that man is superior to woman or even that man's role is any different than woman's. Referring to the previous example, they are simply left-hand and right-hand caretakers of the Garden of Eden.

Where we go wrong is when we think of relationships in terms of who has the power and who doesn't. That's a corruption of God's plan for humankind. Jesus willingly gave up his power in heaven to enter our world as a servant to his Father and a helper to men and women. Every Christ follower – male and female – is called to the same spirit of servanthood.

There is no general call for men to rule over women or women over men. The instruction we are all given is to serve one another. That holds true in every relationship, including marriage. Focusing on who holds the power in a relationship drives a wedge between individuals and tears at the bond of love that should hold us together as God's image bearers.

Why is it that so many turn "`ezer" into a word meaning someone who is subservient when describing the role of a wife or even of a single woman? Chapter 3 holds the key, so stay tuned.

"Let them" rule

As created beings, we humans have only one justification to claim we stand at a higher level than any other part of creation.

According to Genesis, God chose to put His creation in the care of women and men and gave us the inner character to do the job (created each of us in His image).

It isn't that we are stronger or smarter than animals. Many animals are stronger and some of them, at least at times, seem smarter. But only humans have been given a moral responsibility: *"And let them rule over the fish of the sea and over the birds of the sky and over the cattle and over all the earth and over every creeping thing that creeps on the earth"* (Genesis 1:26, NASB). To emphasize the point, these words are repeated in Genesis 1:28-29.

There are plenty of reminders, however, that no human is on a par with God. One such reminder is found in Psalm 8: *"O LORD, our Lord, how majestic is Your name in all the earth, who have displayed Your splendor above the heavens! From the mouth of infants and nursing babes You have established strength because of Your adversaries, to make the enemy and the revengeful cease. When I consider Your heavens, the work of Your fingers, the moon and the stars, which You have ordained; What is man that You take thought of him and the son of man that You care for him? Yet You have made him a little lower than God and You crown him with glory and majesty! You make him to rule over the works of Your hands; You have put all things under his feet, all sheep and oxen and also the beasts of the field, the birds of the heavens and the fish of the sea, whatever passes through the paths of the seas. O LORD, our Lord, how majestic is Your name in all the earth!"* (NASB).

To further clarify who's in charge of what, we can turn to Psalm 115:16: *"The heavens are the heavens of the Lord, but the earth He has given to the sons of men"* (NASB). This leaves no doubt that the heavens belong to God and Earth is delegated to human care. The phrase *"sons of men"* in Psalm 115:16 is translated *"children of men"* in the KJV. The Hebrew word used for "sons" or "children" is "adam," meaning "humanity." The same word, in singular form, is used in Psalm 8:4 and also refers to humans.

Because we know humanity is incomplete unless it consists of males and females, it is a mistake to conclude that Psalm 8:4 and 115:16 mean anything other than humanity – men and women – when they talk about "man" being made a little lower than God.

That 24-hour day question once again

It must have taken a long time for Adam to name all of the living creatures. Is this proof that a day in the garden was longer than 24 hours, as some speculate? Once again, there are arguments for and against this view. I take neither side. I am firmly in the camp of, "It took as long as it took." The time frame is of no concern to me. What matters, as always, is that God created.

Learning how best to fulfill my responsibility for taking care of God's creation is more important to me than knowing how long the creation process took. If we're going to debate, let's focus on how to build closer relationships and how to take better care of the Earth we live on.

Genesis 2:21-23

So the LORD God caused the man to fall into a deep sleep; and while he was sleeping, he took one of the man's ribs and then closed up the place with flesh. 22 Then the LORD God made a woman from the rib he had taken out of the man and he brought her to the man. 23 The man said, "This is now bone of my bones and flesh of my flesh; she shall be called 'woman,' for she was taken out of man."

Much has been written about this portion of Scripture, especially regarding the significance of the man being made first and the woman being made from the man. Better than rehashing all the usual arguments, I think it more helpful to begin with what Moses writes in these first chapters of Genesis and what he emphasizes again in Chapter 5:1-2: *"This is the book of the generations of Adam. In the day when God created man, He made him in the likeness of God. He created them male and female and He blessed* **them** *and* **named them Man in** *the day when* **they were created"** *(NASB — emphasis added).*

Humanity = them = male and female

The words of Genesis 5:1-2 parallel Genesis 1:27: *"So God created mankind in his own image, in the image of God he created them; male and female he created them."* Both chapters make it obvious that God created the first humans in His likeness.

"Created" is used three times in verses 5:1-2. The first time refers to the first man; the next two times "created" refers to both male and female. "Them" occurs three times in verse 5:2. The rest of Genesis 5 eliminates any doubt that all following humans are also created in the likeness of God by giving us a genealogy that runs from Adam to Noah.

Completing our picture of God

With the creation of Eve, the structure of humanity is now complete as male and female. Our picture of God is also more complete. Moses has just told us that humanity — male and female — is what constitutes God's image. Think of the ramifications of that!

Having failed to find his ideal companion among the birds and animals, Adam is full of joy when he wakes and sees Eve for the first time. I believe there is excitement in his voice as he exclaims: *"This is now bone of my bones and flesh of my flesh; she shall be called Woman because she was taken out of Man."*

Some commentators claim verse 23 establishes Adam's authority over Eve because it is Adam who calls her "woman." This is quite a stretch. Everything we've read to here indicates that they are created as partners who share the same commission from God. Besides, in verse 23 Adam does not give the woman a proper name, which actually would infer a claim of authority over her. He merely distinguishes his new wife from himself by referring to her as "woman" ('ishshah) and himself as "man" (ish). "'Ishshah," the feminine form of "ish," is also used to mean "wife."

From here on, the man will be known by "ish" or his proper name of Adam, capital "A." So we have "'ishshah" (woman) and "ish" (man) making up "adam" (humanity). It is now clear that to God, humanity includes (unites) both male and female; humanity does not favor one over the other. Genesis tells us that two individuals – united in their humanity – were placed here as distinct beings, different from all the unconscious and conscious life that preceded them. They had God and each other and they knew their purpose in life.

The world today vacillates between claiming that all humans are one and seeking to divide us into special interest groups that are more and more specific. The more we divide, the more each group fights for power. The more we fight, the more chaotic life becomes. We Christ-followers are called to stand up for unity over division. Scripture tells us that God intends for humans to be united in caring for the Earth and for everything that lives on it, including one another.

Adam, Eve and the image of God

Men and women who ignore the truth of Genesis often struggle to figure who they are and why they exist. Prevailing theories of natural evolution require belief in, as Schaeffer puts it, "a mechanical chance parade from the atom to man, (in which) man has lost his unique identity. As he looks out upon the world, as he faces the machine … he cannot distinguish himself from other things."

A Christ follower need not have this problem. The Bible's assurance that we exist because of a personal Creator gives us confidence that we are not machines. As God's creations, we have the ability to be who we are designed to be each time we step outside our homes and head to work or into the community.

Christians know that what distinguishes humans from animals and machines, says Schaeffer, is that our basic relationship is upward. This differentiation – that we humans are all created in the image of God – makes genuine love possible and gives us unity, even though we are each unique in many ways.

Schaeffer says, "If we are made in the image of God, we are not confused as to the possibility of communication; and we are not confused as to the possibility of revelation, for God can reveal propositional truth to me because I am made in his image. Finally … if man is made in the image of God, the incarnation [God coming to Earth in the flesh] … is not irrational, as it surely is if man sees himself as only a finite being in face-to-face relationship with a philosophic other [an infinite, impersonal everything]."

Where human goodness comes from

Whether we acknowledge it or not, God's goodness and the equal standing enjoyed by creatures made in His image are what form the moral foundation for battling against the mistreatment of all humans (Including those on their way to being born).

Without God, good is a relative term. Those who insist humanity evolved out of nothing, without outside help, can insist that something is right or wrong, but they have nothing solid on which to base their claim. The unconscious matter they believe we "evolved" from can't be either good or bad; it is just a material that can't think or feel or distinguish moral from immoral.

If God's image is not built into us and we don't have His goodness as our unalterable gold standard, morality is a human construction that evolves and shifts over time, like sand in the Sahara desert, blowing this way and that in a capricious wind.

Without God, "is right" is replaced by "feels right," and what feels right depends on current culture and who has the loudest voice within our culture. This type of morality changes with the wind of public opinion and causes the Bible's wisdom to be tossed aside.

Because God never changes, His Word never changes, thus both are viewed as no longer relevant in a self-enlightened and "progressive" modern society.

By way of contrast, when God created our world every part of it met His personal standard for "good." In the first chapter of Genesis alone, God looks at His creation and says six times that it is good. To God, "it is good" is not a relative statement. His definition of good is based on His own purity of spirit, purpose and action and it is a standard that does not change over time.

Because the Bible turns our eyes to God and reveals His eternal goodness, its message will always be the most relevant available to us, regardless of which way public opinion is leaning at the moment.

"I have no problem with anyone's personal faith, so long as it is understood that there are many paths to spirituality and they are all 'correct' in their own manner (obviously not including religions that claim all others are evil and must be destroyed)." – Blogger friend sharing his view of religion

"The relativism which is not willing to speak about truth but only about 'what is true for me' is an evasion of the serious business of living. It is the mark of a tragic loss of nerve in our contemporary culture." – The Gospel in a Pluralist Society, by Lesslie Newbigin, theologian and author

---

Believing the Bible makes one arrogant and/or a fool?

Believing that the Bible is both spiritually and historically accurate often leads to claims that Christ followers are foolish, arrogant, exclusionary, closed minded, judgmental – or all of the above – for not giving equal weight to the beliefs of those who are not Christians.

These charges are unwittingly ironic. Those who make them fail to realize that everyone has his or her own beliefs, whether they fit into a recognized religious system or not. Everyone who holds something to be true is making a judgment that any conflicting belief is not true. People derisive of the Bible also fail to realize that while some of its historical data is not yet proved, none has yet to be disproved.

Complicating the accuracy issue is the claim by some that there is no such thing as truth. If that's true, not even the statement that nothing is true can be true. If there is no truth, we're wasting our time believing in anything or discussing anything. Fortunately, most of us are smart enough to figure out that there are things in life we can know for sure. Touch a hot stove and it will burn us. Step off a high cliff and we go down, not up. Whack a hornets' nest with a stick and we'll be stung. There is a difference between truth and imagination.

It is not logical to single out Christians as arrogant for believing the truth of the Bible when all philosophical and theological beliefs require exclusivity. Even the belief that all beliefs have equal value requires a firm grip on that one tenant, which puts it at odds with every other belief system.

In view of the fact that everyone has some sort of formal or informal belief system and every belief system has precepts that exclude other belief systems, perhaps it is time to stop being unkind to one another and begin looking for ways to have conversations that are more helpful and friendly. Most of us are open to hearing why someone believes what they do. None of us wants to be told we are stupid for not sharing another person's cherished beliefs.

Is syncretism a viable option?

Related to the idea that it is wrong to trust any single religion is the common practice of mixing personal theories of how things ought to be with favorite precepts from various religions and philosophies. This mixing of belief systems is called "syncretism."

Syncretism can be the result of deliberate choice or confusion. One of the arguments for deliberately mixing and matching belief systems is that good people are found among those who claim no interest in anything spiritual, as well as among those who hold to recognized forms of religion. Believing that no religion or philosophy has a lock on the truth, deliberate syncretizers select what they consider to be the best choices from a buffet of religious and philosophical offerings.

While syncretistic beliefs and practices may sound good, they conflict with the teachings of Scripture. The idea of being "good people," for instance, is not the main message of the New Testament or the first three chapters of Genesis. The focus of Genesis 1-3 is on relationships in God's perfect creation and what happens when humans choose to decide for themselves what works best. The main point of the New Testament is God's plan to restore a world that is no longer perfect, because the first humans were wrong when they thought they knew what was best.

The Bible claims to contain *the* truth about God and the world we live in, not *a* truth. Either the book is true or it is not. If it is true, it is not logical or wise to mix in other theologies and philosophies that conflict and, therefore, cannot be true. This Christ follower believes the Bible is true. In the first two chapters of Genesis alone, Moses presents as truth a number of statements that conflict with atheism, humanism, pantheism, Hinduism, Buddhism and other belief systems.

The New Testament contains major conflicts between Christianity and other belief systems. For instance, Jesus is portrayed as God in the flesh (John 8:58, 10:33, 14:9, Mark 14:60-64).

This same Jesus, the Christ, quotes the words of Genesis as a reliable source of knowledge about God's involvement in our world, adding his testimony as to the accuracy of Genesis and firmly linking the Old and New Testaments in space-time history. If we trust the words of Moses and Jesus, as found in the Bible, how can we mix conflicting beliefs from other religions and theologies with scriptures and call the combination "truth?"

The same principle applies to other belief systems. It is impossible to build a coherent belief system on conflicting foundational tenants. It's like building on that shifting Sahara desert sand.

Someone can put up a really great looking structure, but without a firm foundation and sturdy walls, the first big wind will blow it away. Syncretism, then, is the sand that causes mix-and-match belief systems to blow apart under close examination.

Genesis 2:24-25

That is why a man leaves his father and mother and is united to his wife and they become one flesh. 25 Adam and his wife were both naked and they felt no shame.

These verses speak to the solidarity of the relationship God intends for husbands and wives. Previous to this, Adam looked at the woman for the first time and blurted out that she *"is now bone of my bones and flesh of my flesh."* What he said was literally true. Eve was created from his bones and flesh.

Metaphorically, Adam's exclamation illustrates that marriage is much more than buying a license and signing a contract. Marriage is instituted by God, whose intention for this and future marriages is that couples bond together so closely and with such strength that they lose themselves in one another; they become as if they are one flesh.

"That is why," the first words of verse 24, now make sense. Men will leave their parents for the purpose of joining with women in marriage. As in verse 23, the Hebrew word used for man is "ish" (husband/male) and the word for wife is "'ishshah" (wife/woman).

Verse 25 says the two were naked and not ashamed. They had nothing to be ashamed about. God had given them one command and that involved one special tree. Clothing was not optional. Clothes did not exist at this point in history.

Finally, not to beat the point to death, but this section of Scripture is yet another that testifies to Adam and Eve as historical characters, a man and a woman living in space and time. Jesus, in Matthew 19:4-5, refers to Genesis 2:24 as an accurate statement concerning Adam and Eve. This makes it difficult to turn Genesis into a metaphor instead of history.

Are males and females almost – but not quite – equal?

Right about now is when the following thought is often expressed: "Men and women are equal, but God made man to be the head of the woman (hold authority over her), just as Jesus is the head of the church." A lot of really fine Christ followers believe this view reflects God's will. I disagree. For one thing, none of us is Jesus, who most certainly is the "head" of us all by virtue of being there in the beginning (*"In the beginning was the Word [Jesus] and the Word was with God and the Word was God"* – John 1:1). And it is Jesus who serves as our "high priest," as seen in Hebrews 3:1.

On a human level, Adam can hardly be considered the creator of Eve. Adam slept while God pulled a body part out of his side. In essence, God used Adam as a human parts bin. God could have created Eve without using a piece of Adam's body. Why then did He choose this method? I believe God's intent was to provide Adam and Eve – and following generations – with a really memorable object lesson regarding the principle of "one-flesh" unity and mutual need.

Because humanity was not complete until God created the first woman, it seems fair to conclude that men and women not only need one another, we are incomplete without one another. In other words, healthy relationships between women and men, inside and outside of marriage, are necessary if we are to fully reflect the image of God designed into each of us.

When one gender insists on ruling over the other – or retreating from the other – what we see is a failure to realize the male-female unity that God intended when He created Adam and Eve and when he brought them together in marriage. Surprisingly, one Genesis commentary after another finds ways to justify teaching that men have authority over women. Nowhere in Genesis 1 and 2 does Moses say that God defined a male-female hierarchy. Everything he writes refutes that view.

I could understand the headship assumption if God had allowed Adam more of a role in the creation of Eve, but Adam didn't have so much as a clue about the companionship he was missing before God brought Eve into his life.

See Chapter 4 for a discussion of "headship" and "kephalé." How we understand these key words has a direct effect on our relationships with other men and women.

The "who's in charge" debate has a lot in common with what we read in the New Testament Gospels. When Jesus' disciples argue over which of them should be first in the earthly kingdom they think he is about to establish, Jesus responds by telling them: *"The kings of the Gentiles lord it over them; and those who exercise authority over them call themselves Benefactors. 26 But you are not to be like that. Instead, the greatest among you should be like the youngest and the one who rules like the one who serves. 27 For who is greater, the one who is at the table or the one who serves? Is it not the one who is at the table? But I am among you as one who serves."*(Luke 22:25-27).

Matthew 20:25-28 includes the same event, or a similar one, where Jesus tells this to the disciples: *"You know that the rulers of the Gentiles lord it over them and their high officials exercise authority over them. 26 Not so with you. Instead, whoever wants to become great among you must be your servant, 27 and whoever wants to be first must be your slave – 28 just as the Son of Man did not come to be served, but to serve and to give his life as a ransom for many."*

Why humans so often fail

The Bible teaches that we are all failed human beings who find it difficult to be in relationship with Him and with one another, as we were originally designed to be. The next chapter of Genesis provides an explanation for why this is so.

As we've seen in Chapters 1 and 2, the first humans were brought to life in a beautiful place of rest and serenity. They were at peace with God, one another and their environment. What happens in Chapter 3 directly alters all of human history and puts a barrier between us and God. Chapter 3 also explains why all of us who come after Adam and Eve continue to look for ways to recover the sense of peace and serenity our first ancestors lost at the beginning of human history.

The Genesis account of God's original design for humanity and the close relationship He had with Adam and Eve is unique to the Bible, as is the explanation of what broke that relationship.

The New Testament teaches that reconciliation is provided through Jesus, the Christ. He wasn't just a good teacher or a man inhabited by God. He actually was, and is, fully God, who came to Earth in human flesh to reveal Himself to us in a way that could be seen, heard and touched.

It's the principle of the thing

Jesus consistently taught principles instead of rules and regulations. The first principle is that we are to follow him as our Lord and obey him by living for him instead of for ourselves: *"If you love me, keep my commands"* (John 14:15).

Another key "Jesus principle" applies to all human relationships, including those between husbands and wives: If Jesus willingly stepped down from his position in the spiritual realm, if he condescended to serve the very humans he created, we also must be willing to put service ahead of position.

Do you want to be first in your family? Serve your family with all you've got. Do you want to be first at church or in your community? Serve with all you've got. It is not about working our way into God's favor. Because of Jesus, God's undeserved favor (grace) is already available to us. We demonstrate our faithfulness to Jesus by our willingness to serve as he served.

Genesis 2 – Main points summarized

1. The creation stories in Chapters 1 and 2 are different. The first is a global overview that appears to be in chronological order. The second zooms in on God and the humans He creates. Jesus, Paul and Luke verify that the two chapters are not separate stories, but united in their narrative.

2. Genesis 2:1-4 completes the creation story begun in Chapter 1 and God's seventh-day rest establishes a rhythm of work, rest, worship and relationship that is intended to continue to this day.

3. While the Garden of Eden has symbolic meaning regarding eternity with God, it was also a real place, with real plants, animals and people.

4. The seven days of creation may have been 24-hour days or periods of time that were thousands of years apart. That's because the Hebrew word for day (yom) can be specific or indefinite. What we can say for sure is that God created.

5. Jehovah Elohim (Lord God) is the name of the self-existent supreme God who saves and redeems. This name is connected with the idea of salvation for God's people, those He chooses and those who choose Him.

6. Chapter 2 presents a very personal account of the creation of Adam and Eve. Both appear to have come into the world as intelligent adults.

7. Women and men are both created in God's image; plants and animals are not.

8. If humanity consists of males and females, both created in God's image, and humanity was not complete until God created the woman, it seems fair to say that we humans not only need one another, we are incomplete without one another.

9. Neither man nor woman contains the fullness of God; therefore, we humans are not Gods or even gods.

10. Humans are not designed to be self-sufficient. We males and females need Him and we need one another. God designed humans to live on the planet together and to share in the work of caring for the Earth and all that lives on it.

11. Chapter 2 reinforces verses 1:28-29, which establish that it is normal for God to speak to the humans He creates.

12. Genesis 2:16-17 establish God's right to rule over humans, just as Adam's naming of the birds and animals establishes humans as their caretakers. These verses also show that God created humans with a moral sense, the ability to distinguish right from wrong. Verse 17 is the first to mention the possibility of death.

13. Because God designed humans to be in relationship, after forming Adam He created Eve to be *"a helper suitable"* for him. The Hebrew phrase is "`ezer kenegdo." It indicates that Adam and Eve are to be equal but opposite helpers to one another; right and left hands, one no more important than the other.

14. Verses 24 and 25 show us the importance God places on marriage, a union He created. His intent is for each couple to exhibit such a complete unity they become *"one flesh."* To be complete, this one-flesh unity requires both halves of humanity, male and female.

15. The picture of humanity presented in Genesis 2 gives strength to the Christian concept of the unity and purpose of humankind. God's desire is that we unite in love for Him and one another and care for His entire creation, not just the parts we claim to own.

Genesis Chapter 3

Key Thought:

God is real; *therefore, ignoring, disrespecting or disobeying God has real consequences.*

One of my favorite books is *Orthodoxy*, by G.K. Chesterton. What he writes in a chapter titled "The Eternal Revolution" seems a perfect way to introduce Genesis Chapter 3, which deals with the first human sin:

"'Therefore for all intelligible human purposes, for altering things or for keeping things as they are, for founding a system forever, as in China, or for altering it every month, as in the French Revolution, it is equally necessary that the vision should be a fixed vision. This is our first requirement.'

"When I had written this down, I felt once again the presence of something else ... as a man hears a church bell above the sound of the street. Something seemed to be saying, 'My ideal at least is fixed; for it was fixed before the foundations of the world. My vision of perfection assuredly cannot be altered; for it is called Eden. ...'

"Christianity spoke (again) and said, 'I have always maintained that men were naturally backsliders; that human virtue tended of its own nature to rust or to rot; I have always said that human beings as such go wrong, especially happy human beings, especially proud and prosperous human beings.

"'This eternal revolution, this suspicion sustained through centuries, you (being a vague modern) call the doctrine of progress. If you were a philosopher you would call it, as I do, the doctrine of original sin. You may call it the cosmic advance as much as you like; I call it what it is – the Fall.'"

Chesterton's words refute the modern progressive belief that an impersonal "nature" is causing humans to evolve toward some undefined future perfection. He reminds us that if improvement is to take place, there must be a standard toward which we strive. Chesterton then asks: "If nature is impersonal, where does this standard come from?"

For Jews and Christians, our standard of perfection is found in the first two chapters of Genesis. God made the heavens and the Earth and all the life within and it was good. Stars, planets, Earth, humans and animals were all behaving exactly as God intended.

Here in Chapter 3, however, Moses provides a vivid illustration of humans deliberately choosing to move away from perfection; away from the God who created them. As a consequence, we are not evolving toward future perfection; we are heading toward chaos. And we are about to discover what happens when perfection collides with free will.

Genesis 3:1-4

Now the serpent was more crafty than any of the wild animals the Lord God had made. He said to the woman, "Did God really say, 'You must not eat from any tree in the garden'?" 2 The woman said to the serpent, "We may eat fruit from the trees in the garden, 3 but God did say, 'You must not eat fruit from the tree that is in the middle of the garden and you must not touch it, or you will die.'" 4 "You will not certainly die," the serpent said to the woman.

To understand the rebellion against God that is about to happen, keep in mind that God created Adam and Eve as free humans. They are able to choose between obeying the one rule He gave them or facing the consequences of ignoring that one rule. There is nothing programmed about their behavior.

What's this about a talking serpent?

The Garden of Eden is God's perfect work and Satan – having already rebelled against God prior to this time – is not in the garden when Adam and Eve are placed there, so who or what is the serpent?

It appears to me that the serpent mentioned here is an animal that belongs in the garden, but which is used by Satan. This means that Satan came into the garden from the outside to inhabit or corrupt the serpent. Could the serpent actually be Satan? Yes, but God is about to punish the serpent in a way that appears to separate it from Satan.

There is no specific mention of Satan in Genesis 3. It is other Bible references that tell us he is the agent of Adam and Eve's downfall. He is the one who wants to see humans join him in rebellion against God and he's the one leading a war against his Creator. Isaiah 14:12-15 explains what Satan's rebellion is about and Revelation 12:9 refers to Satan as a serpent: "*The great dragon was hurled down – that ancient serpent called the devil, or Satan.*"

I believe Satan speaks to Eve through this "crafty" serpent. The Hebrew word for "crafty" is "arum," which can also be translated as "cunning or subtle." There's a bit of a word play going between Genesis 2:25, which tells us that Adam and Eve were naked and innocent (arom) and 3:1, which says the serpent was cunning (arum). The two words are opposites that sound very much the same. The serpent is no dummy. That's probably why Satan uses it. Because the serpent is in the Garden of Eden, I assume it started out good, like everything else God placed there. Satan himself is brilliant; he was once one of the most magnificent beings in the supernatural world. It was by Satan's choice, not God's, that he ended up rebelling against his Creator.

Supernatural or super naive?

The unseen spirit realm that some view as a naive Christian fantasy is real. It isn't off in space somewhere; it is all around us. Perhaps that is why nearly all belief systems recognize the spiritual world, including Islam, Hinduism, Buddhism, paganism and atheism.

The supernatural is every bit as natural as the universe we can see and there is a cause and effect relationship between our world and the supernatural. If we refuse to acknowledge the existence of the unseen portion, we can't expect to understand our seen world.

In Genesis 3:1-4, Satan moves from the unseen world into the seen world of space-time history. This is not some cartoony guy in a red devil suit. He is a dangerous, powerful angel who is at war with God. He is also at war with us. Once again, I don't believe this is a metaphor for evil entering the world. This is really Satan coming into contact with a real woman and real man.

The Hebrew word translated as serpent is "nachash," which in its most common form means serpent or snake. The name is thought to have come from the hissing sound made by a reptile. Bible commentator Adam Clark looks at all the ways the word has been used historically and concludes that it appears to be "a sort of general term."

He writes that the original word is construed by the ancient Greek translation of the Old Testament (the Septuagint) as a serpent not because this was its fixed meaning, but because it was the best that occurred to the translators. What else can we discover about "nachash" from the text? The serpent's understanding, or craftiness, was superior to that of other animals. It may have walked upright before being cursed. It could speak and reason, at least in this instance.

Focus on the message, not the messenger

Some commentators write that Eve would have expressed surprise if it was unusual for the serpent to talk. I'm not sure that is a fair inference. Who can say what Eve accepted as normal? Her "normal" certainly wasn't our normal.

Whatever or whomever Eve spoke with in the garden, that's not the important aspect of the event. What matters is the choice made by Eve and Adam as a result of the temptation placed before them. When we focus on the questions that aren't answered instead of the ones that are, it is easy to get sidetracked and miss the lesson. It is also easy to dismiss this as a fairy tale because of the talking serpent aspect.

We humans easily get caught up in tales of the supernatural when they involve Harry Potter, Luke Skywalker, Superman and vampires, but we find it extremely difficult to accept a biblical description of a real supernatural event. Perhaps the entertainment industry has done us a disservice by depicting the supernatural in ways that allow us to lose our minds to fantasy, while obscuring the seen and unseen reality that surrounds us.

What next, a talking mule?

Do you find it difficult to deal with the possibility of a talking serpent? If so, you're not alone. Let's see if we can resolve our doubts by looking at the story of yet another talking animal. This one is found in Numbers 22: 27-29, the account of Balaam and his donkey: *"When the donkey saw the angel of the Lord, it lay down under Balaam and he was angry and beat it with his staff. 28 Then the Lord opened the donkey's mouth and it said to Balaam, 'What have I done to you to make you beat me these three times?' 29 Balaam answered the donkey, 'You have made a fool of me! If only I had a sword in my hand, I would kill you right now.'"*

The verses from Numbers don't solve the reality versus metaphor question yet, but they will, thanks to the Apostle Peter, a man Jesus personally chose as one of his representatives. When explaining how God chastised Balaam in 2 Peter 2:16, the apostle writes: *"But he was rebuked for his wrongdoing by a donkey — an animal without speech — who spoke with a human voice and restrained the prophet's madness."* Peter's words are unmistakable. The donkey, *"an animal without speech,"* really *"spoke with a human voice."*

If God can use a donkey to speak to a man, it should not surprise us that Satan can speak through a serpent.

The supernatural is admittedly difficult to deal with, but we don't have to understand everything there is to know about that realm; we just need to accept that it exists and realize that beings who inhabit the supernatural world make themselves known in our world from time to time. God and others of the unseen world are not bound by human expectations of what can and can't be done. They sometimes choose to speak to humans in ways that rattle our senses.

Perhaps Satan spoke to Eve through the serpent because Eve was used to seeing it and appreciated its beauty. He would then be approaching her through something she liked and felt comfortable with. Whatever the reasons for giving voice to animals, the Bible says at least one serpent and one donkey really spoke.

The Fall begins by questioning God

Up to now, the Garden of Eden has been absolute perfection. There is no evil anywhere and Adam and Eve have no reason to fear death because it is not yet part of their world.

Then Satan approaches Eve as the serpent or by speaking through the serpent. Notice that Satan begins with a question: "Did God really say not to eat of the tree?"

Can you hear the skepticism? Eve knows the answer; either God told her or Adam did. At any rate, Eve is about to face humanity's first moral challenge: Do I obey God or my own desire? She tells the serpent that God said not to touch or eat of the tree or she will die. We don't know if God added the "don't touch" part or Eve did. It doesn't matter. What counts is Satan's response, which essentially is: "Trust me on this. You won't die."

Satan is emphatic in his contradiction of God. He wants Eve to doubt God's wisdom and trustworthiness. He wants her to be discontented with who she is and where she lives. He wants her to desire the same power as that possessed by God. What Satan doesn't tell Eve is that he knows there is a real and serious penalty for disobeying God. He has already experienced it. Obviously, Satan wants Eve to fail as he did.

Genesis 3:5

"For God knows that when you eat from it your eyes will be opened and you will be like God, knowing good and evil."

Learning to distinguish good from evil suggests having the wisdom and authority to determine what is right and wrong. Because only God has both, Adam and Eve opened the door to a problem that exists to this very day. We humans want to determine for ourselves what is right and wrong. We want to be our own authorities.

The pull of desire was strong for Eve, as it is for us. What is it like to know what God knows? What is it like to experience evil? If God loves me, will He really punish me for eating from the tree of the knowledge of good and evil? How much can it hurt me to take one little bite? Faced with temptation, Eve hesitates. Satan then drags out his biggest lie of all (my paraphrase): Eve, you can be like God! You have a choice. Just reach out and take from the tree!

God didn't tell Adam and Eve they would become like Him if they ate fruit from the tree; He said they would die. Satan not only lies to eliminate this danger, he is crafty enough to shape his lie so it has the most appeal. But maybe it is more simple than that. Perhaps Satan just figured that Eve is like him and if Satan wants to be like God, so will she.

A lesson from the book of Steinbeck

One of my all-time favorite novels is *East of Eden,* written by John Steinbeck. Steinbeck did not claim to know God, but he understood human nature, as do all the best novelists. Steinbeck's book is an updated version of Cain and Able, a story that comes a little later in Genesis.

In the Steinbeck book, one brother envies and torments the other, all the while feeling that he is born bad and has no choice in the matter. Without giving away the ending, the Hebrew word "timshel" (or "timshal") is translated as "thou mayest" and plays a significant role.

I thought of *East of Eden* as Eve reaches a crossroads here in Chapter 3 and God gives her freedom to choose her path. "Thou mayest" applies to her, as it does to us every time we are offered a choice. Choose to obey God or choose to disobey. None of us is programmed. We're not puppets on a string. We're not machines. "Thou mayest."

Satan wants Eve to rebel, knowing she will be banished from God's presence, just as he was. That's a truly ugly sentiment. This appears to be the first instance of a behavior we still see today, one that causes unhappy humans to hope for – or even cause – others to fail. A loving person who is going through a painful time does not want anyone else to experience their pain. Yet we see that people who are troubled, often deliberately or unconsciously set out to make others as unhappy as they are. Could Satan's lie to Eve be the origin of the aphorism, "Misery loves company?"

Eve is already gifted by God with a perfect companion in a perfect paradise. She and Adam have everything they need for a perfect and very long life. All they are told to do is to stay away from one tree – a tree whose beauty they can enjoy from a distance and whose fruit is not important to their happiness or survival. But we humans are rebellious, aren't we? Don't ever tell us we can't have something that is within our reach. Do that and all of the sudden we find ourselves obsessing over the thing we don't have, while minimizing the value of what we do have.

It is not surprising so many women and men feel that choosing for ourselves is better than listening to God. We live in a world where millions defy Him and don't die any faster than those who seek to obey God. Many of these God-defiers become rich and famous by pursuing the very things the Bible tells us will result in death. The consequences are there, though, even if they are not obvious to outside observers. There are always consequences to disobeying God.

Satan's big lie is based on us wanting what we can't have

Satan's big lie to Eve stands as the foundation for all other lies. His big lie says that we humans, we who are created, can be equal with our Creator. It would be wonderful to say we've learned from Adam and Eve over the centuries, but history shows that human personalities really haven't changed. We still find reasons to reject God's love. We still want to possess God's power and authority and exert it over others. We still find it difficult to be satisfied with who we are and what we have, especially when something desirable seems out of reach.

It is because Adam and Eve bought into Satan's lies that God has given us a longer list of commandments than they were given. They had only one. By the time God gave His commandments to the nation of Israel through Moses, there were 10. The 10th, in Exodus 20:17, is *"You shall not covet."* Coveting what does not properly belong to us is the basis for many of our sins. Satan's lies worked with Adam and Eve because it didn't take much to convince them that they needed what God possessed.

When Jimmy Carter was President he responded to a reporter's question about what he'd done wrong in his life by saying that he had lusted (coveted) in his heart. That simple statement set off gales of public laughter and much mocking, including hundreds of jokes on late-night TV. In reality, Carter's theology was spot on. Paul wrote in 2 Corinthians 11:3: *"But I am afraid that just as Eve was deceived by the serpent's cunning, your minds may somehow be led astray from your sincere and pure devotion to Christ."*

Coveting often begins in our hearts and minds long before we act. Because thought is often the precursor to deed, Jesus teaches that our thoughts – or heart condition – may subject us to judgment (Matthew 5:21-22 & 27-28).

Eve's sin begins in her mind and then translates into action. For this reason it is appropriate to say that her sin occurs the moment she believes Satan instead of God.

Some clarification is needed here. It is not sin to be tempted. Jesus was tempted by Satan, but we are told he did not sin (Luke 4). Sin does not come from the temptation, but from embracing the temptation, thinking about it, pondering the possibilities and even taking steps closer to the reality of it.

Perhaps this emphasis on what is happening inside of us (in our hearts and minds) explains why Jesus does not follow the Ten Commandments with an even longer list of dos and don'ts for right living. Instead, he distills the commands of the Law into two main principles: Love God with all your heart, soul, strength and mind and love your neighbor as yourself (Mark 12:30-31). He teaches that everything we do must flow from these principles. This requires that we make daily choices to give love a higher priority than our own desires.

What we think, who we listen to, what we read and what we watch all give shape to who we are as people and influence how we behave. Adam and Eve listened to Satan and bought into his lie that they could be like God. Watch what happens next.

Genesis 3:6-7

When the woman saw that the fruit of the tree was good for food and pleasing to the eye and also desirable for gaining wisdom, she took some and ate it. She also gave some to her husband, who was with her and he ate it. 7 Then the eyes of both of them were opened and they realized they were naked; so they sewed fig leaves together and made coverings for themselves.

Eve takes a close look at the tree of the knowledge of good and evil and is impressed. She sees its beauty and, no doubt, thinks how great it will be to possess God's wisdom. Seeing nothing but the benefits, she rejects God's command and eats from the tree.

Where is Adam when Eve needs him?

Not everyone agrees with my view, but it appears to me that Adam is right beside her. He stands silently and watches, perhaps waiting to see what will happen to his wife, the one he has so joyfully welcomed into his life not all that long ago.

It is surprising that many commentaries fly right past, *"She also gave some to her husband, who was with her."* They build entire theologies for male-female relationships based on a belief that Adam, the strong, wise male, was not present to protect Eve, the weak, easily fooled female, from Satan's appealing arguments.

One egregious example is from the otherwise helpful *Whole Bible Commentary Critical and Explanatory,* by Jamieson, Faussett and Brown: "[Eve was] the object of attack, from Satan's knowledge of her frailty, of her having been but a short time in the world, her limited experience of the animal tribes and, above all, her being alone, unfortified by the presence and counsels of her husband. Though sinless and holy, she was a free agent, liable to be tempted and seduced."

The Believer's Study Bible finds, "The woman in her sin did indeed usurp the headship of the man; whereas the man was no less guilty, as he abandoned his leadership when he 'heeded' the voice of his wife."

Is the image of God weaker in Eve than Adam?

There are problems with the previous comments about the weakness of Eve. Everything we have read thus far – before the Fall – makes it plain that Adam and Eve are equal in every way. They are both made in the image of God and both carry the same responsibilities as caretakers of the earth.

To state, based on what we've read to here, that Eve usurped "the headship of the man" is poor interpretation. Even worse, to impute weakness and foolishness to Eve because she is a woman is tantamount to imputing the same weakness to God. Remember, she is made in God's image.

Furthermore, no place in the text does it indicate that Adam was not present with Eve. Verse 6 gives the impression that Eve took the fruit and ate, turned and handed some to Adam. The

Hebrew word for "with" is "im." It is a preposition that means against, along, among, aside, close and together.

When Moses writes that Adam was "with" Eve, the text says to me that Adam was in close proximity to her. Verse 6 does not tell us that Eve picked the fruit, ate it and then searched out Adam so he could take a bite. In my opinion, to explain the verse as these two commentaries do is to imitate Adam. They point at the woman as the cause of sin, instead of accepting the reality that both Adam and Eve failed to live up to their shared responsibilities.

Adam was three times silent

The Silence of Adam, a book by Crabb, Hudson and Andrews, notes that Adam's sin began with silence. "He listened to the serpent, he listened to his wife, he accepted the fruit and then he ate. Adam was passive three times before he ate the forbidden fruit. God's speaking brought creation out of chaos; Adam's silence brought chaos back to creation. Adam used silence to destroy relationship. God rested after His creative work; Adam labored harder as a result of his silence."

While I find it difficult to read past the book's several references to Adam as "the image-bearer" (instead of "an image bearer"), the conclusion about Adam's silence and its results provides a lot to think about concerning when to be silent and when to speak. As the authors share in *The Silence of Adam*, "Speaking is the gateway to relationship. Silence is the gatekeeper. Words usher us out of silence and connect us to God." Their conclusion is that "Adam taught us what not to do."

Finding encouragement

Another thought-provoking book by Larry Crabb and Dan Allender is *Encouragement: The Key to Caring*. It came to mind when I was meditating on the verses in Genesis 3.

Encouragement, as illustrated in their book, is essential in human relationships. When struggling with life, we need the encouragement of others who will stand beside us and offer strength. Adam and Eve were both weak at the same time and that led to disaster.

I attend church regularly to worship God, share life with other Christ followers and find encouragement. I realize that churches can be messy and terribly frustrating. That's to be expected. Churches, like every other assembly of humans on Earth, are filled with flawed people. But it's amazing how much good we can do for one another when we decide to encourage rather than remain detached or point fingers and find fault.

The decision-making process

The example of Jesus' life shows us that every major decision is best made when preceded by prayer. Adam and Eve didn't have that example, as we do, but they could have talked to God face to face if they had waited for Him to join them in the garden.

Instead, we find Adam standing silently beside Eve, noting that she took a bite from the fruit and didn't drop dead. Thus encouraged, when she turns and offers the fruit to him, Adam also takes a bite.

The immediate result is to notice they are naked, a condition that did not bother them until now. Puritanism is thousands of years in the future, so we can't say they are being puritanical. Something real is happening here and it isn't just about clothing or the lack thereof. The consequences for all future humans and even animals and the Earth itself, are staggering.

Satan's whopper proves you can't always have it your way

One important truth Adam and Eve are about to learn is that a just and loving God has no choice but to judge between right and wrong, good and evil. God's judgment always involves at least two aspects: (1) Our choice to obey or disobey Him and (2) His decision as to how He applies justice while leaving the door open to reconciliation, which is His constant desire.

God is not the originator of sin, nor does He tempt people to sin. That's on Satan, as seen in James 1:13, but Satan didn't force Adam and Eve into rebelling against God – he didn't have to.

How does Satan succeed? He appeals to Eve's desire to know what God knows and says, in effect, "Trust me, you won't die. God doesn't want you to know what He does. Knowledge is power and right now God has it all. You can be like Him and it will be great!" (My paraphrase.)

Satan knows that the most effective lies are those that contain a mix of fact and fiction, so he adds a pinch of truth. Here, the truth is that Eve will gain knowledge about evil through this personal experience. Unfortunately, as Schaeffer notes, it is a "useless, horrible knowledge!"

When pots imagine they are the potter

Some very bright men and women place such a premium on their own minds and their own experiences, they feel comfortable concluding that God has nothing to offer them. What they fail to realize is that they are repeating, yet again, the mistake that altered the flow of human history.

God is always God, regardless of what we think. He is infinite, all powerful and unconstrained by time and space. Having created our world, He can add to it, alter it or make it disappear. We have no such power and even the most intelligent among us can't avoid the personal "expire-by" dates that limit our time on Earth, nor can we alter the truth about life after death. When the time comes to face our Creator, I wonder how many of us will think of the verses that follow and want to hide.

Genesis 3:8-13

Then the man and his wife heard the sound of the Lord God as he was walking in the garden in the cool of the day and they hid from the Lord God among the trees of the garden. 9 But the Lord God called to the man, "Where are you?" 10 He answered, "I heard you in the garden and I was afraid because I was naked; so I hid." 11 And he said, "Who told you that you were naked? Have you eaten from the tree that I commanded you not to eat from?" 12 The man said, "The woman you put here with me—she gave me some fruit from the tree and I ate it." 13 Then the Lord God said to the woman, "What is this you have done?" The woman said, "The serpent deceived me and I ate."

If we focus on the act of eating a piece of fruit from a forbidden tree, we miss what is really going on. God gives us the freedom to be in relationship with Him or to reject Him. These are the only two choices: with or against.

The ability to choose between listening to God or our own personal desires was built into Adam and Eve, just as it is for each of us. By their disobedience, they showed that being in relationship with God, at least for a time, was not as important to them as indulging in their impulses. After eating from the tree, however, both quickly realized they had made a bad choice. The proof is what happens when they hear God walking toward them in the garden. For the first time ever, they try to hide from Him.

With rebellion comes consequence

Adam and Eve understand that what they did was wrong and they don't want their moral failure (their sin) to be seen by God. In Genesis 2:25, we're told Adam and Eve were naked and not ashamed. What a contrast we see here! Instead of feeling free, they are hiding their shame, covering their bodies and trying to avoid God.

Before eating from the tree, God was their friend and companion. Now, because of a bad moral choice, there is a barrier between them and God, literally and figuratively.

After the rebellion – for that's most certainly what it was – Adam and Eve feel fear, not friendship. Keep in mind that these are not mythical humans hiding from a theological concept. We're speaking of a human male and a human female, trying to hide from the very real creator of the universe. When God asks Adam why he is hiding, Adam responds that it is because he is naked and scared.

God next asks, *"Who told you that you were naked? Have you eaten from the tree that I commanded you not to eat from?"* Look how quickly Adam forgets about Eve and goes into personal-protection mode. His response is that the woman *"you put here with me"*made me disobey you. So much for marital unity. Eve is on her own.

When God asks Eve what she has done, the response is that the serpent deceived her. Neither takes responsibility for his or her own actions. Both are quick to point fingers, even at God Himself.

By their actions, Adam and Eve set the stage for relational dysfunctions that exist to this day. Humorist James Thurber wrote a book called, *The War Between Men and Women.* The title sums up one of the results of this first sin. Adam's shout of joy when he first saw Eve has turned into discord, division and blame. For the first time ever, men and women are engaged in a type of warfare.

The guilt Adam and Eve feel, even as they try to pin the blame on someone else, is both real and appropriate. Guilt and alienation are the first of several serious consequences of their rebellion. This alienation, as we are about to see, will affect every aspect of our world.

One powerful illustration of alienation in this age is that we humans are divided by gender, race, religion, age, national origin, sexual preference and every other way we can think of. No nation is immune from these relationship issues. Alienation may have begun in the Garden of Eden, but it now covers the globe.

We're so divided we classify some acts as "hate crimes," because it is somehow more heinous to assault or murder a human who is not in one's own special interest group than to do the same to one who is. This view of life is about as far from the perfection of Eden as we can get. In reality, because all humans carry the image of God, every crime is a hate crime.

Genesis 3:14-15 (NASB translation)

The LORD God said to the serpent, "Because you have done this, Cursed are you more than all cattle and more than every beast of the field; On your belly you will go and dust you will eat All the days of your life; 15 And I will put enmity Between you and the woman and between your seed and her seed; He shall bruise you on the head and you shall bruise him on the heel."

The serpent used by Satan now receives a curse from God. The Hebrew word for curse is "arar." It carries the expression of great loathing and bitterness. God is really, really upset. He gave everything to Satan, and to Adam and Eve, and still they wanted more.

There's a Greek word that describes this covetousness, this lust for more. It's "pleonexia" (pronounced pleh-on-ex-ee-ah). After the first sin, "pleonexia" is such a problem that coveting

becomes a major theme throughout the Bible. New Testament
mentions include Luke 12:15, Romans 1:29, Ephesians 4:19,
Ephesians 5:3, Colossians 3:5, 1 Thessalonians 2:5 and
2 Peter 2:3.

The curse is real – and it is symbolic

The curse in verse 15 is symbolic of the penalty that God places
on Satan himself, but God also places a curse on the serpent that
is both severe and real. Unfortunately, Moses does not explain
why God chooses to punish the actual animal. Perhaps it is so
the serpent will serve as a living reminder of this terrible event.
Perhaps the serpent could have prevented itself from being used
by Satan. We just don't know.

God's real-world curse is twofold. The first is that there will
forever be hostility between the woman and the once admired
serpent. The second is that it will crawl on its belly from here on.
Some take this to indicate that the serpent once walked upright.
What we can be sure of is that crawling on its belly would not be
a curse if that was how it originally traveled.

The word translated as "cursed" in this verse (arar) appears
twice in Chapter 3; here for the serpent and in verse 17
regarding the ground. Adam and Eve face difficult new
consequences, but they are not personally cursed. God does
not remove the blessings or responsibilities He gave them in
Genesis 1.

Moses' messianic metaphor

The statement in Genesis 3:15 that there will be hostility
between Eve's seed and the serpent's seed contains a prophecy
about how God will bring an end to the war between Himself
and Satan. Note this phrase: *"He shall bruise you on the head and
you shall bruise him on the heel."* God is speaking to Satan (the
serpent). The "he" God refers to is Jesus, the Messiah who will be

born of a woman, but without the seed of a man (Luke 1:35, Galatians 4:4).

The bruising of Jesus' heel is the crucifixion. Here God is telling Satan and his followers that despite the horrific violence they will inflict on Jesus, they will only wound him temporarily. On the other hand, the resurrection of Jesus will administer a wound to Satan that leads to the death of him and his followers, and eternal life for the followers of Jesus (Revelation 20:10). Interestingly, the fatal wound inflicted by Jesus is not from responding to violence with violence; it comes from Jesus' ability to absorb the violence of Satan, die and return to life.

Another Messianic prophecy about Jesus is found in Isaiah 53:9-12: *"He was assigned a grave with the wicked and with the rich in his death, though he had done no violence, nor was any deceit in his mouth. 10 Yet it was the Lord's will to crush him and cause him to suffer and though the Lord makes his life an offering for sin, he will see his offspring and prolong his days and the will of the Lord will prosper in his hand. 11 After he has suffered, he will see the light of life and be satisfied; by his knowledge my righteous servant will justify many and he will bear their iniquities. 12 Therefore I will give him a portion among the great and he will divide the spoils with the strong, because he poured out his life unto death and was numbered with the transgressors. For he bore the sin of many and made intercession for the transgressors."*

Hebrews 2:14-15 links Jesus to the prophecy written in Isaiah roughly 800 years earlier, displaying, yet again, the unity of the Old and New Testaments: *"Since the children have flesh and blood, he too shared in their humanity so that by his death he might break the power of him who holds the power of death – that is, the devil – and free those who all their lives were held in slavery by their fear of death."*

Why we need a reboot

Humans once had free and direct access to God. When Adam and Eve sinned, that free access was cut off. We humans can only stand in the presence of the God of perfection if we are morally perfect. Because Adam and Eve brought sin to the entire human race, none of us qualify.

Their rebellion against God means that a restart is needed to set things right between Him and humans once again. God chooses that this restart will come through Jesus. He is seen in scripture as a type of "second Adam;" one whose role is to repair what the first humans broke.

Wiersbe's Expository Outlines on the Old Testament says this about the second Adam: "Romans 5 and 1 Corinthians 15:42-49 explain the contrasts between the first Adam and the Last Adam, Christ. Adam was made from the Earth, but Christ came down from heaven. Adam was tempted in a perfect garden, while Christ was tempted in a terrible wilderness. Adam deliberately disobeyed and plunged the human race into sin and death, but Christ obeyed God and brought righteousness. As a thief, Adam was cast out of paradise. Speaking to a thief, Jesus said, 'Truly I tell you, today you will be with me in paradise'" (Luke 23:43).

Genesis 3:16

To the woman he said, "I will make your pains in childbearing very severe; with painful labor you will give birth to children. Your desire will be for your husband and he will rule over you."

The KJV translates God's words to Eve this way: *"I will greatly multiply thy sorrow and thy conception; in sorrow thou shalt bring forth children."* This phrase uses two Hebrew words to indicate pain or sorrow. The first is "itstsabon" and the second is "etseb." Both come from the same root that *Strong's Hebrew Dictionary* defines as "worrisomeness, that is, labor or pain: sorrow, toil." *Strong's* defines "itstsabon" as a pain or toil and "etseb" as labor or sorrow.

I believe God is telling Eve that the birth process, which was not originally intended to be long and difficult, will bring two types of pain. The first pain, "itstsabon," is physical. The second, "etseb," is best seen in the KJV translation of this phrase: *"in sorrow thou shalt bring forth children."*

God is warning Eve that bringing children into the world, from conception through birth, is going to be a lot harder as a result of disobeying Him. The potential death of mother, child, or both, now enters the picture and adds an emotional pain – or sorrow – to physical pain. On top of that, there are the sorrows Eve and her children will face in a world that is no longer perfect. God's prophesy becomes a reality in the very next chapter. After Eve successfully gives birth to Cain and Abel, it doesn't take long before the elder brother murders the younger and multiplies the sorrows of the first family.

Because Eve wanted to be like God, she and the parents who come after her will feel the same type of sorrow God feels when babies die, illness hits, families face difficult life circumstances that are not of their own making and when His children make bad choices. None of this is part of God's original design.

Is "he will rule over you" a game changer for women?

The next part of Genesis 3:16 – *"Your desire will be for your husband and he will rule over you"* – is also more complicated than it appears at first glance. If you've been wondering why there's an on-going power issue between men and women, this sentence is where it originates.

In his book, *Genesis in Space and Time*, Francis Schaeffer acknowledges the initial equality of men and women. Then he explains the last line of Genesis 3:16 this way: "This one sentence puts an end to any unstructured democracy. In a fallen world unstructured democracy is not possible. Rather, God brings structure into the primary relationship of man, the man-woman relationship." He writes, "In a fallen world, in every relationship, structure is needed for order. Form is given and without such form freedom would only be chaos." That form, according to Schaeffer, is male headship.

As much as I admire Schaeffer's book about Genesis, I believe he misses the mark on this verse. There can be no restart, no return to God's original design for relationships between men and women, if we claim Jesus as Savior, yet our lives continue to reflect a male-female authority structure based on the consequences of sin. For more about Eve's desire for Adam and him ruling over her, see the discussion of Genesis 3:20.

Reconciliation begins now, not in the future

When God told Eve that Adam would rule over her, it was the result of the broken relationships between the humans and God and between the man and woman. Adam ruling over Eve in the marriage relationship was not God's original design; it was a consequence of their sin, as Schaeffer acknowledges.

Adam and Eve's own moral failure drove a wedge between them. That was then; this is now. Why would any Christ follower want to stick with a dysfunctional structure that is the result of ignoring God when He offers us the opportunity to return to His perfect original plan?

Jesus makes it possible for us to begin living as God designed, reconciled to Him and to one another. Here's what Paul wrote in Colossians 1:19-20: *"For God was pleased to have all his fullness dwell in him [Jesus] and through him to reconcile to himself all things, whether things on earth or things in heaven, by making peace through his blood, shed on the cross."*

The life of Jesus, both in words and actions, speaks volumes about how to restore the unity among humans that was damaged by the first sin. Jesus began by flipping his culture's established roles for males and females upside down. How, you ask? For starters, he accepts women into his band of disciples. He welcomes them into his presence and teaches them just as he does the men.

Here's what Jesus told two women followers, Mary and Martha, as related in Luke 10:38-42: *"As Jesus and his disciples were on their way, he came to a village where a woman named Martha opened her home to him. 39 She had a sister called Mary, who sat at the Lord's feet listening to what he said. 40 But Martha was distracted by all the preparations that had to be made. She came to him and asked, 'Lord, don't you care that my sister has left me to do the work by myself? Tell her to help me!' 41 'Martha, Martha,' the Lord answered, 'you are worried and upset about many things, 42 but few things are needed —or indeed only one. Mary has chosen what is better and it will not be taken away from her.'"*

In the culture of that time, men and women normally did not mix. Women existed to serve the men, were not formally educated and most had virtually no standing outside their own homes. Martha complains that Mary is not fulfilling her traditional role as one who serves the men. Jesus tells Martha that her sister is taking the better road by sitting at his feet and listening to his every word.

Another example involves the mutual hatred between Samaritans and Jews. No respectable Jewish man would be seen talking to a single woman in public, let alone a Samaritan woman, and most certainly not a Samaritan woman with a troubling history. Yet, in John 4:5-42, we read that Jesus has a quiet conversation with just such a Samaritan woman that not only transforms her life but turns her into an evangelist. Her words bring the entire community out to hear him teach.

An even more stunning encounter between Jesus and a woman disciple occurs after the crucifixion. In John 20, the apostle tells how Mary Magdalene comes to the tomb early on the third day, while it is still dark. This Jewish woman was possessed by demons until Jesus healed her. Thanks to him, Mary's life changed dramatically and she became one of his most devoted followers.

Jesus appoints the first post-resurrection evangelist

Going to Jesus' tomb after the crucifixion, Mary is shocked to see that it is open and empty. She races to find Peter and John (*"the other disciple, the one Jesus loved"*) and the three run back to the tomb. John provides a glimpse into his own humanity by letting us know that he ran fastest.

When the two men go into the tomb, Mary stays outside, weeping. This is when the resurrected Jesus approaches her. Surprisingly, she does not recognize him, perhaps because of her tears. Or maybe it's the shock of seeing him alive after watching him die three days earlier on a Roman cross (No one ever got off a Roman cross alive).

Finally, after Mary realizes who she is talking with, Jesus gives her an assignment: *"Go to my brethren and say to them, 'I ascend to My Father and your Father and My God and your God'"* (John 20:17, NASB).

This verse didn't fully grab me until one Easter Sunday at church when our pastor, Jake Hendrix, pointed it out. Who does Jesus choose as the first person to see his resurrected body? A woman. Not just any woman, one who had been inhabited by demons! Jesus could have stepped past Mary and spoken to Peter and John. They were two of Jesus' closest friends and disciples. That would have been the expected thing to do in most cultures, not just their patriarchal Roman and Jewish societies. Instead, Jesus seeks out Mary Magdalene.

It was during Jake's telling of this space-time account in the lives of Jesus and Mary that I realized I've been blind to her story for decades. In first-century Israel, women were not allowed to give witness in a court of law, nor were they allowed to speak to a man in public. What the Gospel of John tells us is that Jesus deliberately chooses Mary Magdalene as his first post-resurrection evangelist (someone sent out to testify about the risen Christ) and tells her very specifically, *"go to my brethren."*

This is remarkable. Mary Magdalene is being sent to tell men the Good News! Unlike the cultural expectation in the first century, her testimony isn't just acceptable to Jesus, she is who he wants as his witness.

Lest anyone think Jesus is sending Mary to the women of her community, the Greek word John uses for "brethren" is "adelphos." It means literally "a brother" or figuratively "much like a brother."

The risen Christ is throwing a cultural taboo to the ground with a resounding CRASH! He is sending Mary Magdalene to men to testify about his resurrection. The significance of this should not be ignored or minimized.

Back to the future

Jesus is teaching us how to behave as reconciled humans in a fallen world. In doing so, he is showing us that he does not expect male-female relationships to continue on as they were before he came to live on Earth.

Choosing Mary to carry his message to the apostles is the act of someone who is deliberately resetting male-female relationships back to God's original design, to where they were before the Fall. This should not surprise us. Jesus came to restore all creation to its original design. Male-female relationships are a high priority in the restoration process, as Jesus demonstrates.

In his book on Genesis, Francis Schaeffer writes that the Fall made necessary a hierarchy that puts women under the rule of men. He makes patriarchal rule sound positive and necessary. ("Form is given and without such form freedom would only be chaos.") Sadly, his view about maintaining the post-Fall patriarchal structure is a widely-held opinion among commentators, pastors and parishioners, despite what Jesus taught and did.

I know this is repetitious, but we keep getting it wrong, so here it is again: Everything in Genesis prior to the Fall shows that God designed women and men to be united in their love of Him, His creation and one another. Prior to the Fall, there was not a hint of male-female hierarchy.

The sin of Adam and Eve resulted in severe consequences, not the least of which was that husbands began to rule over their wives. It didn't take long before that consequence of sin grew into men ruling over women, period.

Why defend the cultural status quo when Jesus didn't?

The example Jesus left us with is quite different. He demonstrated his great love by giving up power and authority in order to serve the very people who should have fallen down at his feet in worship. Instead of allowing himself to be served, Jesus got on his hands and knees to wash the feet of his disciples, an act of love that shocked and confused them (John 13:1-17).

Foot washing was a job reserved for the lowliest of servants. It was unthinkable that a host wash feet, let alone that a rabbi such as Jesus would humble himself this way.

Our Lord also allowed himself to be beaten, mocked and hung on a cross like a common thief. His acts of love make any debate about who has the authority over whom in a marriage, or any other relationship, seem terribly petty by comparison. If Jesus modeled love and service over power and control, perhaps it is time to stop debating and start following our Savior.

Genesis 3:17-19

To Adam he said, "Because you listened to your wife and ate fruit from the tree about which I commanded you, 'You must not eat from it,' cursed is the ground because of you; through painful toil you will eat food from it all the days of your life. 18 It will produce thorns and thistles for you and you will eat the plants of the field. 19 By the sweat of your brow you will eat your food until you return to the ground, since from it you were taken; for dust you are and to dust you will return."

God has already told Eve how she will pay for her rebellion. Now Adam finds out the consequences of his disobedience. First, God tells Adam that the ground is cursed because he listened to his wife and ate from the tree. This is huge. It marks a change in the natural world that goes well beyond what will happen to Adam. The relationship between humans and the Earth is now broken.

As part of God's curse, the land will give life to thorns and thistles, things that apparently did not exist before the Fall. The second half of the curse is that Adam is fired from his cushy job as a caretaker in the Garden of Eden, where food grew for the taking and safe shelter was provided.

Now Adam will have to work hard to provide what he and his family need to survive. He will fight not only the Earth itself but weather, animals and other hazards in an environment that is no longer perfect.

In verse 19, some translations say, *"you will eat bread."* Does this verse introduce an entirely new food that didn't exist before or does "bread" mean food, as is indicated in other translations? In Genesis 1:29-30, when God is telling Adam about the plants and fruits he can eat, the word used for food is "oklah," which means food or meat.

The word for bread here in Chapter 3 is "lechem." "Lechem" can be used to mean bread, grain, or, in a broader sense, food. Why Moses chooses "lechem" over "oklah" is unclear, but it is possible he is indicating that Adam will soon learn how to grow, process and bake grain. The main message, however, is that food will not be as easily available as before the Fall.

Is marriage still important?

On the way to unpacking Adam's consequences, it is easy to miss the information contained in verse 17: God said to Adam, *"Because you listened to your wife."*

I am resisting the urge to joke here because there is a serious point to make. God's use of "wife" confirms that the marriage union created in Chapter 2 comes directly from Him. Despite what many in our culture believe, marriage is not an old-fashioned social convention that is no longer relevant.

There will come a time when marriage will no longer be needed, as Jesus teaches in Luke 20:34-36. That time will arrive when Jesus returns to finish the good work already begun on Earth. Until then, marriage continues to be important and our role in a marriage relationship is to love our husband or wife so completely that we are constantly putting the interests of our spouse ahead of our own.

This concept makes many men and women uncomfortable. The expectation in our current Western culture is that we will maintain our individuality and put our own desires first, no matter what. The angst this causes when single men and women consider marriage is one of the most frequently repeated themes in novels and movies.

A related theme is the destruction caused by men and women who try to maintain their independent, self-focused lives after marriage. Interestingly, happy Hollywood endings often lead to married couples realizing that they must become partners, each giving up something of self to benefit the other.

Does Genesis, or anywhere else in the Bible, teach that every man and woman must marry? Not at all. What we're told is that when men and women do marry they are to form a union that is meant to be exclusive and lasting. The failure of a high percentage of marriages in our time is not evidence that God's intent is misunderstood or rendered obsolete. Marriages fail because we live in an imperfect world full of imperfect humans.

Evolutionary biologists report in

It is fascinating to read what "evolutionary biologists" write in relation to marriage. One such biologist is C. Owen Lovejoy, a well-known researcher and author, whose often-quoted article, "The Origins of Man," was published in *Science*, in 1981. Lovejoy wrote that male-female bonding in lasting pairs was the critical step in human evolution and is something built into us by nature. To Lovejoy and those who believe as he does, this "nature" is always an impersonal force that does what it does without thought or emotion.

What confounds me is how an impersonal "nature" can build anything into humans. Building in requires thought and purpose, something an impersonal force is not capable of. Humans, on the other hand, are quite capable of building bias into most things, including approaches to scientific studies.

An example, it seems to me, is the title "evolutionary biologist," which builds a bias into modern biology. This label leans strongly in the direction of the theory of evolution by "natural" selection first proposed by Charles Darwin in 1859.

Evolutionary biologists may say they are free to go wherever their studies take them, but trying to find a university biology department that acknowledges the possibility of a Creator is like trying to locate Bigfoot. There are rumors, but actual sightings are hard to come by.

Regardless of any potential biases among evolutionary biologists, however, by confirming that male-female bonding is critical to humanity, science is once again catching up with what Moses wrote in Genesis 3,400 years ago.

Also found in Genesis and throughout the Bible, are numerous examples of what happens when men and women do not bond according to God's original design. While scientists struggle to understand why women and men have so much trouble getting along, Christians (including those in the sciences) look to the Fall in Chapter 3 to explain where our problems began.

"Nature" is our sister, not our mother

The word "nature" implies a personal, creative power that maintains consistency throughout our universe. There is nothing random about the "laws of nature." Their consistency is what allows us to trust scientific experiments, all of which rely on a "nature" that does not permit chemical elements to change their behavior over time, whether separately or when combined with one another.

G.K. Chesterton writes quite a lot about nature in his classic book, *Orthodoxy*. He says, for instance, that, "The world might conceivably be working towards one consummation (one ultimate completion), but hardly towards any particular arrangement of many qualities … Nature by herself may be growing more blue; that is a process so simple that it might be impersonal. But Nature cannot be making a careful picture made of many picked colors unless Nature is personal.

"If the end of the world were mere darkness or mere light it might come as slowly and inevitably as dusk or dawn. But if the end of the world is to be a piece of elaborate and artistic chiaroscuro, then there must be design in it, either human or divine.

"The world, through mere time, might grow black like an old picture, or white like an old coat; but if it is turned into a particular piece of black and white art, then there is an artist. ... An impersonal force might be leading you to a wilderness of perfect flatness or a peak of perfect height. But only a personal God can possibly be leading you (if, indeed, you are being led) to a city ... in which each of you can contribute exactly the right amount of your own color to the many-colored coat of Joseph."

Chesterton further writes, "Only the supernatural has taken a sane view of Nature. The essence of all pantheism, evolutionism and modern cosmic religion is really in this proposition: that Nature is our mother. Unfortunately, if you regard Nature as a mother, you discover that she is a stepmother. The main point of Christianity was this: that Nature is not our mother; Nature is our sister.

"We can be proud of her beauty since we have the same father, but she has no authority over us; we have to admire, but not to imitate. ... This, however, is hardly our main point at present. ... Our main point is that if there be a mere trend of impersonal improvement in Nature, it must presumably be a simple trend towards some simple triumph."

A consequence of sin is death

After the Fall, the nature of life changed from simple to a lot more complex, especially because death was introduced as a consequence of Adam and Eve's sin. It does not appear that death was part of God's plan for men and women, but it is now a reality for all of us.

We who descend from Adam and Eve inherit the consequences of their sin, which is why our days on Earth are also limited.

The difference for us is that Jesus presents us with the gift of his life. By choosing to follow him as our Lord and Savior, we can reconcile with our Creator and overcome the death sentence.

Creation is no longer at peace

Before the Fall, the Garden of Eden had boundaries and both human and non-human life existed peacefully within them. This raises an obvious question: If all was peaceful in the garden, what was happening outside in the rest of the world? Without revelation from God or an account from a historian such as Moses, we can only guess. What we know is that the changes Moses is describing in Genesis Chapter 3 affect all relationships within our world. Not only is the Earth going to make life difficult for humans, animals and humans are going to make life harder for one another.

Genesis 3:20

Adam named his wife Eve, because she would become the mother of all the living.

On the face of it, Adam's naming of Eve is a simple act, but a closer look brings up a number of questions. For instance, why Eve and not something else? When Adam calls his wife Eve this is actually the third name applied to her. Like the first man, Eve is initially known as "adam," because she is one half of the male-female combination that comprises humanity. This God-given generic name comes with a God-implied ideal that men and women who marry will form a unity that is so strong the two will be as "one flesh." One flesh, one name: "adam."

Eve's second name is "'ishshah" or "woman." Like "adam," this is also a generic label. "Woman" has meaning because there is a "man" to serve as a counterpart and vice versa. Her role is to stand alongside Adam as his equal partner. Finally, there is

"Eve," the name given to her by Adam after the Fall. The Hebrew word for "Eve" is "Chavvah," meaning "life." This is an interesting juxtaposition to the previous verse, which speaks of death.

Digging deeper into the naming of Eve

Is Adam thinking about the life the two will have together and the lives that will come into the world through Eve? Keep in mind that Adam and Eve already know they are to populate the Earth (Genesis 1:28).

Does Adam realize his life is incomplete without his companion? Does the name he chooses – life – celebrate her existence? Or can it be that he is unwittingly providing a prophetic view into the future, when Eve will give life to the one whose descendant will crush Satan, thus doing away with the far-reaching effects of Adam and Eve's first sin? The answer to why Adam chose that name may be one of the above, both or something entirely different. We just don't know.

Furthermore, the second half of verse 20 is also perplexing. Moses writes that Adam gave her this name because Eve *was the mother of all the living.* Using the past tense in reference to Eve as the mother of all the living seems inappropriate before she is a mother for the first time.

But the ancient Hebrew text can also be translated as The International Standard Version (ISV) does. It says Adam named his wife Eve because *she was to become the mother of everyone who was living.* The New Living Translation is similar: *she would be the mother of all who lived.*

Yet another puzzle is why the naming of Eve occurs at this point in the narrative. Adam and Eve have just learned from God that they face serious consequences as a result of their disobedience. It is an odd time for Adam to think about naming his wife.

Dr. David Timms wonders if there is a sinister reason behind Adam's choosing this moment to name Eve. Dr. Timms is dean of the Faculty of Theology/School of Christian Leadership at William Jessup University, in Rocklin, California. He says that "until this point in Genesis, Adam has named only the animals (at the Lord's invitation) to establish his dominion over them. In Jewish culture, the one who names has authority over the one who is named. Hence, parents have authority over their children, etc." "Is it possible," Dr. Timms asks, "that this abrupt act from Adam, immediately on the heels of the curses being pronounced, is a grasp for power and authority in Adam's relationship with Eve?"

Adam takes control

Dr. Timms' question helped me rethink these verses and consider the following: Because Adam and Eve ate from the forbidden tree, God asserted His authority over them. When someone exercises authority over us, it is not unusual to look for ways to regain control of our lives by seeking to exert control over someone or something else. This can lead to mastering a job, a hobby, a sport, a person, a group of people or anything that fulfills the need to be in control.

Adam is a typical human who wants to control his own life, but God is taking away a great deal of his former freedom. What could be more natural than for Adam to jump at this opportunity to name Eve and claim authority over her; to establish his power over her? This explanation seems logical when we realize that the relationship between Adam and Eve began to crumble the moment they disobeyed God. When personal relationships are not built on mutual love and trust, competition for power and control frequently takes over.

Now add to the equation that Adam has just overheard God telling Eve that her desire will be for Adam and "*he will rule over you.*" What isn't clear is whether God's statement to Eve prescribes what He wants to happen between Adam and her or whether God is predicting what will happen now that sin has entered the world. My view is that God is expressing sorrow (predicting). He knows Adam will seek to rule over Eve and this will introduce all sorts of difficulties into male-female relationships for centuries to come.

To rule or not to rule, that is the question

While I take the position that God is giving Adam and Eve a look into the future – and Adam is making a power grab – many theologians and pastors teach that God is prescribing male headship as the preferred relational model. They believe that Adam was always intended to rule over Eve.

After the Fall, they say, Adam recognizes his failure to keep Eve from sinning, accepts responsibility for failing to guide (control) her, takes up his tarnished mantle of headship, names the woman Eve and, by doing so, makes certain she understands he intends to regain his authority over her. Their logic for claiming Adam's authority over Eve is that:

1. Adam was created first.

2. Adam was the source of Eve.

3. Woman was created for the sake of man, as his helper.

4. It was Adam who named the first female "woman," thus asserting his God-given authority over her.

Those who follow this train of thought also use the New Testament as a foundation for interpreting the Old, which, it seems, puts the cart before the horse. Genesis 1 and 2 reveal God's perfect original design. Those chapters provide the foundation for understanding God's intention for male-female relationships. Chapter 3 explains what went wrong. The New

Testament describes the restoration process begun by Jesus and which, by necessity, included overthrowing the patriarchal culture that came into being after the Fall.

Looking at the four points noted above, the idea that Adam was made before Eve is irrelevant. One could just as well argue – though I am not doing so – that Eve had authority over Adam because God created conscious life in ascending order: sea creatures, birds, land animals, Adam and then Eve.

If Eve's source is Adam, his source is …

The idea that Adam was the source of Eve is also difficult to support. Adam didn't know he needed a mate, didn't know how to make one and was asleep when God took the body part that was used to create Eve. Besides, if Adam is her source (the material she is made from), it logically follows that dirt is his source. But we know that dirt (or clay) is just a material used by God, who is the source of both Adam and Eve.

The third point, that Eve was created for Adam, requires a closer look. Genesis 2 tells us that God's intent was to make a *"helper suitable"* (`ezer kenegdo) for Adam. As we have noted, the Hebrew text reveals that this is not a one-sided arrangement. Each person comprises half of what is necessary to constitute humanity, thus humanity is not complete until God creates both male and female. Adam and Eve are equals but opposites; right hand joined with left hand to serve God and one another – at least until the Fall pits right hand against left hand.

Regarding the fourth point, it is a mistake to believe that Genesis 2:23 means Adam is claiming authority over Eve when he calls her "woman." Adam sees that God's newest creation is not a fish, bird or animal. She is a human like him and Adam recognizes that the male half of humanity now has a female counterpart. Her proper name is not "woman" any more than his proper name is "man."

When we add what we know about God's original design to what we know about the way Jesus treated women, the weight of the argument is heavily against the idea of male headship as God's perfect design for humanity.

More thoughts concerning a biblical view of male and female roles follow in this chapter and the next two.

Desiring Adam

Before moving on, let's revisit this portion of verse 16: "*Yet your desire will be for your husband and he will rule over you.*" The Hebrew word for desire is "teshuqah" (tesh-oo-kaw). It means to stretch out after; to crave or long for someone or something.

A straightforward reading of this verse makes sense to me, as it apparently does to Eugene Peterson, who translates it this way in *The Message*: "*You'll want to please your husband, but he'll lord it over you.*" Even though their relationship is now broken, Eve is still Adam's wife. She will still desire him, despite the fact that he will seek to establish control over her and, at times, make her life difficult.

Mary Jensen, a friend from our church community group, offers the following insight that goes in a different direction than Peterson's translation, but, I believe, is equally on target. Mary says, "This verse makes me think about many women I know, including myself, who desire a more personally intimate relationship with their husbands. The complaint is often that the husband works too much; work comes before family, etc. This phrase from Genesis makes me wonder if it is telling us that wives will desire that close companionship once so idyllically known in the garden when Adam, Eve and God walked together and chatted in the cool of the evening. That ideal was ruined with the Fall, when Adam had to start dealing with thorns and sweat on his brow."

A closer look at the meaning of "teshuqah"

The Hebrew word for "desire" (teshuqah) only appears three times in the Old Testament. The second use is in Genesis 4:7, which we will get to in a moment. The third use is in Song of Solomon 7:10, where "teshuqah" carries the sense of sexual longing.

Some believe Genesis 3:16 also has a sexual connotation. Others see "desire" as indicating an emotional dependence on Adam, Eve being thought the weaker of the two. Yet another view is that as a result of God's judgment, women's desires will naturally be completely subservient to those of their husbands. Any woman not desiring to be subservient will be acting in an unnatural, or ungodly, way.

In most of these views, it is assumed the man was always intended to have authority over the woman. What changes after the Fall, according to these explanations, is that the man morphs from gentle ruler into tyrant.

A bridge too far

One line of thought regarding male headship that I find most disturbing is based on the way "teshuqah" is sometimes interpreted in Genesis 3:16. This interpretation says that after the Fall women will seek to rule over men, but men must resist, just as they must resist all forms of sin.

Those holding this view get it primarily from Genesis 4:7, the second use of "teshuqah," where God tells Cain: *"If you do what is right, will you not be accepted? But if you do not do what is right, sin is crouching at your door; it desires to have you, but you must rule over it."*

In this verse, God uses an illustration that personifies sin, gives it a human nature. He does this to warn Cain that he must master his sinful desires. If Cain doesn't learn to rule over sin, he will become its slave. The parallel some create with Genesis 3:16 is to say that a woman has the same desire to rule over her husband as sin has to rule Cain and a man must master his wife in order to avoid becoming her slave.

Even though the same word for desire is used in Genesis 3:16 and Genesis 4:7, the context is obviously not the same. Sin was never intended to be Cain's marriage partner. God Himself brought Adam and Eve together in marriage. In verse 16, God tells Eve her desire will be for (or to) her husband; He does not say that her desire will be against Adam.

There is nothing in Genesis Chapters 1-3 to make me believe that God punished Adam and Eve by condemning them to a war over power, even though such a war between men and women is still being fought today. One gender – or one spouse – trying to rule the other is contrary to God's original design and is the opposite of how Jesus modeled love and servanthood.

The war over power comes from not loving one another as Jesus loves us. It is Christ-like love that becomes the game changer and puts us back on the track to healthy, happy relationships. When we focus on love in a relationship, the question of who should hold the power is no longer an issue.

Genesis 3:21

The LORD God made garments of skin for Adam and his wife and clothed them.

Adam and Eve cover themselves with leaves. God then makes them (or shows them how to make) garments from an animal hide or hides. There is more to think about here than the idea that clothing now becomes a necessity.

Some see clothing as a symbol of Adam and Eve's disobedience to God and the eventual covering of our sin with the blood shed by Jesus on the cross. In any event, all relationships on Earth are now broken, including those between humans and animals. Animals and humans once lived together peacefully in the garden. God is now sacrificing an animal, or animals, to provide clothing for Adam and Eve.

Later, in Genesis 9:2-3, God tells Noah: *"The fear and dread of you will fall on all the beasts of the earth and on all the birds in the sky, on every creature that moves along the ground and on all the fish in the sea; they are given into your hands. 3 Everything that lives and moves about will be food for you. Just as I gave you the green plants, I now give you everything."*

Not only is peace replaced with fear and conflict, animals and humans begin to compete against one another for food and animals become food for humans. Later, God will also instruct humans to use animals as sacrifices to Him until Jesus comes to Earth and becomes the one sacrifice that never needs repeating.

Genesis 3:22-24

And the Lord God said, "The man has now become like one of us, knowing good and evil. He must not be allowed to reach out his hand and take also from the tree of life and eat and live forever." 23 So the Lord God banished him from the Garden of Eden to work the ground from which he had been taken. 24 After he drove the man out, he placed on the east side of the Garden of Eden cherubim and a flaming sword flashing back and forth to guard the way to the tree of life.

Adam and Eve were not created to rival God. They were to be His companions. Like Satan, however, Adam and Eve wanted to know all that God knows – to be equal with God – and now, like Satan, they are banished from God's presence in paradise. The major consequence of disobedience to God, then, is estrangement from Him and, eventually, death (eternity apart from God's love).

The moment Eve grabbed the fruit of the forbidden tree, she broke her relationship with God and handed herself the death sentence. The same was true for Adam. God didn't make them disobey. He's the one who warned them not to eat the fruit.

To prevent Adam and Eve from regaining their lost immortality by eating from the tree of life, God sends them out of Eden. The tree of life was not forbidden to them previously because eating from it before they sinned would not have changed a thing; they were designed to live forever.

Yes, I know it sounds crazy to say a human can live forever, but that is because of how we've been conditioned to think over the centuries. Why is the concept of human immortality more weird than the idea that the basic building blocks of life suddenly appeared out of nowhere. Or that, without help, inanimate materials accidentally created a beautifully ordered universe, with consistent natural laws and complex living organisms, including humans who have the capability to study the accidents that created them out of nothing?

In my view, the lifespan of matter depends on the Creator, as does the lifespan of humans. What is there, other than faith, to provide scoffers with a sense of certainty that much longer lives – even eternal lives – are impossible?

The God who saves and redeems

Genesis 3:24 says, *"He drove the man [human] out."* The Hebrew word for "drove" is "garash," which means to expel, but can also give the sense of divorce. The God of justice and mercy is keeping His word. He is doing what He warned Adam and Eve He would do if they disobeyed the one law He gave them. There are always consequences to our disobedience, just as there is always a path back to God, as Moses indicates here by using *"Lord God"* to refer to our Creator.

As noted in the earlier discussion of God's name, *"Lord God"* indicates that our Creator is the eternal supreme God who saves and redeems. I believe Moses uses *"Lord God"* twice in verses 22 and 23 to make sure we get the message that even though God is sending Adam and Eve out of the garden, He still loves them and desires to redeem them (buy them back; make things right with them).

"The man has now become like one of us" appears to be a lament. Once again, "man" is humanity (adam with a lower case "a"). Note also another reference to "us" (the Trinity). Jamieson-Faussett-Brown's *Commentary on the Whole Bible* translates verse 22 this way: *"Behold, what has become [by sin] of the man who was as one of us!"*

Reading this exclamation as an expression of sympathy or sadness makes sense. Adam and Eve were perfect and were created to live forever. They were not gods; they were God's creations, designed to be very much like Him. What do you think? Is God expressing compassion, anger, sadness or some of each in verse 22?

When He sent Adam and Eve out of paradise, they went into a land that was no longer at peace, but it was not to a place that made life unbearable. And God was not without a plan for helping them find their way back to Him.

Cherubim, real or imaginary?

To prevent Adam and Eve, or future generations, from moving back into the Garden of Eden, God posted angelic guards called "cherubim." The Hebrew word for "cherubim" is "kerub." The same word is used to describe real beings, as well as imaginary figures. Ezekiel 28:14 makes it clear that Satan was this type of real figure when it says: *"You were anointed as a guardian cherub."* Here in Genesis, Moses appears to indicate that the cherubim are also real angelic beings.

Are we learning from history or repeating it?

Adam and Eve's new life outside the garden was very different from when God created two perfect humans and placed them in a perfect environment. By eating from the forbidden tree, Adam and Eve learned more than they bargained for. They experienced moral guilt, distress, blame, sorrow and the breaking of all their relationships. They would eventually add death to that sorry list.

You'd think we humans, having centuries of experience to draw on, would learn from the lessons of the past. We pride ourselves on being more intelligent than our ancestors and we have access to more knowledge than our ancient ancestors ever dreamed of, yet we continue to say yes to Satan. How much smarter are we, really?

Genesis 3 – Main points summarized

1. Chapter 3 explains why the world is not perfect and we humans are not perfect. Contrary to modern progressive thought, "nature" is not causing humanity to progress toward some undefined future perfection. The standard of perfection for the Earth and all living things – including humanity (men and women) – is found in the first two chapters of Genesis, before rebellion against God entered the world. In this current time, as in earlier centuries, we continue to suffer the results of ignoring, disrespecting and disobeying our Creator.

2. Adam and Eve were created as free humans, able to choose between obeying the one command God gave them or disobeying that one command. God's authority to rule over them and the rest of his creation was established in Chapters 1 and 2. He did not leave it to the humans to figure out for themselves what was right and wrong; He gave them a built-in moral compass and clear instructions.

3. God is not the originator of sin. He gives us the freedom to obey or disobey (thou mayest). The choice is ours. The catch is that there is always a consequence to disobedience and these consequences often affect others, not just ourselves.

4. When Satan crossed from the unseen spirit realm into the seen world and appeared to Adam and Eve, the idea of disobedience (rebellion) entered the world for the first time. Satan is not a metaphor or theological concept; he is a real enemy of God and all humanity.

5. Satan's goal, as always, is to cause us to fail. When Satan told Eve that eating from the forbidden tree would open her eyes and give her the ability to decide for herself what was best for her, he was telling her that God is not trustworthy. He was challenging God's character and authority.

6. Desiring what we don't have – coveting – is at the root of many sins. Satan's big lie is that we humans will be better off if we ignore our Creator and make our own life decisions, regardless of what God tells us. In other words, Satan wants us to covet God's authority and strive to live independent of God's influence.

7. Coveting usually begins in the mind (or heart) long before we act. Perhaps this is why Jesus taught principles rather than rules and regulations. Everything Jesus taught flows from these two core principles: Each of us is to love God with all our heart and soul and love our neighbors as ourselves.

8. God and other members of the unseen world sometimes use surprising means to communicate with humans. In Genesis, Satan appears as a serpent or through a serpent. In Numbers, God speaks through a donkey. In Exodus, God speaks to Moses through a burning bush. In Acts 9, God speaks to Paul as a light from heaven flashes around him. Most amazing of all, the New Testament Gospels tell of God entering our world as a human baby and living with us for roughly 33 years.

9. God created Adam and Eve as equal partners in His new creation. When they disobeyed God they were equally guilty. Though Eve was first to eat the forbidden fruit, Adam was standing next to her waiting for his turn. If Adam bears extra guilt, it is because he stood silently by and watched Eve sin before he himself sinned.

10. Many Genesis commentators teach that Eve was weak, naive and susceptible to sin because she was a woman. The first three chapters of Genesis, however, make no such claim about the first woman. Genesis says that both Adam and Eve were made in the image of God.

11. The consequences of Adam and Eve's sin are staggering. The world is no longer at peace. There are broken relationships

everywhere we look: between humans and God, between humans and other living creatures, between humans and the Earth. The worst consequence for Adam and Eve was that they no longer enjoyed a comfortable relationship with God. Before God ever confronted them about their sin, they felt so much fear and shame that they tried to hide. The first consequence of disobedience, therefore, is estrangement from God.

12. God's judgment always involves two choices: (1) Our choice to obey Him or not and (2) His choice as to how He applies justice. Here at the beginning of human time, we see an early hint that God is ready with a plan to bring us safely back into His family after we make wrong choices, if we choose to come home.

13. Relationships are sustained by loving God and loving one another. Sin breaks relationships. Adam blamed God and Eve for his own disobedience. Eve blamed the serpent. This is a pattern that continues to this day. Blame games and power struggles have been dividing men and women ever since the Fall.

14. God curses the animal we call a serpent and condemns Satan to eventual death through a man born of woman. God does not curse Adam and Eve, though He bans them from the Garden of Eden, makes their lives more difficult and takes from them the privilege of spending eternal life in the garden with Him.

15. Humans once had free and direct access to God. When Adam and Eve sinned, that direct access was cut off. We humans can only approach our perfect God on our own if we are perfect. Because Adam and Eve brought sin into the world, none of us qualify as perfect. Adam and Eve's rebellion against God requires a restart to set things right again. Genesis 3 contains a prophetic reference to how that reboot will take place.

16. The life of Jesus demonstrates how to repair relationships between men and women. In actions that completely turned their cultural expectations upside down, Jesus welcomed Mary

as a disciple; chose a Samaritan woman to evangelize her village; and chose a woman who had been inhabited by demons as his first post-resurrection evangelist. If these are not examples of how to behave in a reconciled world, why are they such prominent stories from the life of Jesus? Jesus not only tore down cultural barriers, he reset male-female relationships back to God's original design. A related thought: If Jesus deliberately chose women to spread his Good News, perhaps we ought to take a second look at Scriptures we think are meant to prevent women from taking active leadership and teaching roles in our churches and Christian organizations.

17. God tells Adam the ground is now cursed because of sin. This marks a change in the natural world that affects everyone and everything. Even plant life and the behavior of animals change (Genesis 3:17-19). Adam and Eve are forced to leave the cozy confines of the perfect Garden of Eden and make their way in a world full of thistles and thorns.

18. Marriage is important because God makes it so. The Genesis 3:17 reference to Eve as Adam's wife testifies that God Himself formed this first marriage bond. Add to it Genesis 2:21-24 and we find that our picture of God's intention for marriage is more complete. No place in Scripture are we told that men and women must marry. When they do, however, their unions are intended to form bonds that are so close they become as if they are one flesh. It is also interesting to consider that man by himself did not present a complete picture of the image of God, nor would woman by herself. It was only by uniting the two that we see male and female personalities forming a single strong bond, one that allows a special type of love and communication. God's design for humanity is for men and women to work together as caretakers of the Earth, loving each other and living in harmony. Humanity is not all male or all female; it is both.

19. The ultimate consequence of sin is death. Does this mean that some lives are eternal and some end? My understanding is that life is eternity in the presence of our Creator, who is the source of all love. Death is eternity outside the presence of God, where there is no love. There can be no joy or sense of fulfillment in a world filled with pain and suffering and completely devoid of God's love.

20. From Adam and Eve to this modern age, we humans are still falling for the same satanic lies. We still want to be God and we are still paying the consequences.

Chapter 4

Key Thought:

Jesus and his apostles reshaped the traditional roles of men and women, *returning them to how things were before sin entered the world. This chapter looks at New Testament passages that illustrate how he and his apostles began to repair the relational fractures caused by the sin of Adam and Eve.*

In the roughly 1,400 years between when Moses wrote the Book of Genesis and Jesus walked on the Earth, males dominated every aspect of society. Jewish and Gentile single women, for example, were subject to the authority of their fathers. Married women obeyed their husbands.

If a widow had a son, she was often subject to him, as the reigning male in her family. Women could not participate in the political process or give witness in a legal action. They were taught household skills but usually did not receive any sort of formal education.

When men got together, women were kept separate, except to serve the men. While it was relatively easy for a man to divorce his wife according to civil and religious laws, women found it almost impossible to get away from bad situations caused by their fathers, husbands or sons.

In ancient China, women's roles were similarly linked to their families. Women were defined as daughters, sisters, wives or mothers. At all times, they were under the dominion of men. When young, it was their fathers. Later, husbands took control.

If widowed, here also sons replaced husbands as the male authorities over them. Women's roles, whether they were in Confucian, Taoist, Buddhist or Hindu societies, were much like those in the Jewish and Gentile societies.

Before we look at how Jesus and his followers treated women, it is important to keep in mind that around the globe the roles of men and women had been mostly unchanged for centuries. Even now, 20 centuries after Jesus, women still don't fare much better in some cultures.

Compare women's roles in current-day Saudi Arabia and on the African continent with ancient times. In Saudi Arabia, where the legal system is based on Sharia law, women were allowed to vote for the first time in August of 2015.

As of 2018, women still need the permission of a guardian to marry and cannot do such "normal" things as open a bank account, go anywhere in public without a male chaperone or try on clothes in a store. If a woman disobeys her guardian, she can be arrested on charges of "disobedience." More importantly, obtaining a life-saving medical procedure requires the written signature of a male relative and a woman's testimony in court is worth only half that of a man's, which makes a woman's ability to get a fair trial suspect.

In Africa, writes Paul Vallely, "Women work two-thirds of Africa's working hours and produce 70 percent of its food, yet earn only 10 percent of its income and own less than 1 percent of its property. They work three hours a day longer than the average British woman does on professional and domestic work combined." (Vallely is a senior research fellow at the Brooks World Poverty Institute at the University of Manchester. He writes for the *New York Times* and other publications.)

The good news for Jewish women centuries ago was that their men (fathers, husbands and sons) tended to treat them better than men treated women in many other cultures. In most Jewish homes, husbands valued their wives more than any other "possession." But valuing women did not prevent Jewish men from beginning each day with prayers from the Talmud that thanked God they were not Gentiles, slaves or women. (The Talmud is a collection of writings that covers Jewish law and tradition, compiled and edited over many centuries, both before and after Christ.)

Sadly, being valued as a possession is a far cry from being valued as an image-bearer of God.

Where did the seemingly universal idea come from that males were meant to dominate?

When determining how to live in the world, Jewish priests and scholars began with the basic supposition that the religion of the Old Testament was the highest and best of all. It was to them, they reasoned, that the one true God, Jehovah Elohim, had revealed Himself as He had to no other people. This gave the Jews an inside track on figuring out how to best live according to God's desires.

Yet despite direct revelation from God to the Jews, male-female roles under Jewish law and within the Jewish culture looked a lot like the male patriarchies in nations that followed other gods or no gods at all. Were the ancient Jews and other world cultures adapting to a natural evolutionary process when forming their strongly patriarchal societies or was there an event in history that universally affected – and still affects – human relationships?

We've already seen the Bible's answer to that question in Genesis 1-3, which is why those chapters are so important as a foundation for understanding God's original design for male and female roles.

Our oldest ancestors, as we know from Genesis, rebelled by choosing to ignore the one command initially given to them by God. That rebellion led to all sorts of broken relationships and tore apart the God-designed, one-flesh unity between Adam and Eve. Instead of living as equal partners, united in their love of God and one another, Adam claimed authority over Eve. We're told in Genesis 3:16 that God Himself predicted the mess Adam's decision would create.

True to form, we humans ignore God's original design and continue to blame Him and one another for our failures, just as Adam and Eve did. We are created in God's image, but we don't want to be like Him. We want to be our own gods; we want to be Him. The root of our problems, I believe, is our ongoing rebellious desire to determine for ourselves what is right and wrong. It is this rebellion that leads to broken male-female relationships over time and across cultures.

Ironically, each generation thinks it is smarter than – and morally superior to – each preceding generation, while continuing to re-enact the original sin of Adam and Eve.

God's plan to reconcile women and men

God's plan for His creation does not include an eternity of dysfunction caused by humans who think we know what is best, even if our ideas of "best" differs from those of our Creator.

Chapter 3 of this book describes how Jesus began the process of reconciling men and women to God and one another. The starting point was Jesus' willingness to step down from his place of honor in the heavenly realm to become a servant to the very men and women he created.

Jesus never sought earthly power, nor did he ever use his heavenly power to force men or women to obey him. But when it came to the established cultural rules of the patriarchal society he lived in, Jesus did not hesitate to flip them upside down in order to demonstrate how he wants us to live.

In the previous chapter, we saw examples from his life that included: how Jesus welcomed women into his circle of "learners;" his respect for women; the compassion he showed for both women and men; and his choice of a woman as the first person to carry the news of his resurrection to his male disciples – even though two male friends were only steps away. Jesus was interested in resetting human relationships back to God's original design, not in perpetuating the patriarchal nature of his culture.

Instead of instituting a new type of relational hierarchy or reinforcing the one in effect throughout the Christian and non-Christian world, Jesus taught basic principles to men and women that can be summarized this way:

• Love God

• Love your neighbors

• Unite around your love of my Father and me

• Serve one another as I have served you

When we read the instructions given to his followers, they are never gender specific and there is no hierarchy, no need to struggle for power. Christ is King and we are his followers. It is that simple.

Why then do the same old relational issues continue to plague us? I believe we have yet to see significant change because we live in a world full of humans who haven't heard, or who choose to ignore, the message of reconciliation that Jesus brought us.

Even those of us who claim to be his followers continue to argue over who God has commissioned to have authority (power) over whom. No doubt Jesus watches with sadness and wonders why we won't pay attention to his personal example.

Jesus prays for his disciples

In his Gospel, John tells of Jesus praying for his disciples and those who would become his disciples. Jesus says this to his Father: *"I have given them the glory that you gave me, that they may be one as we are one – I in them and you in me – so that they may be brought to complete unity. Then the world will know that you sent me and have loved them even as you have loved me"* (John 17:22-23).

Jesus makes no distinctions regarding gender. He prays for all of his disciples (student-followers), who we know included both men and women. The unity he speaks of refers to much more than gaining equal access to salvation. Unity includes equal access to the spiritual gifts and ministries God provides to build and nourish His church.

Parable of the sheep and goats

In Matthew 25, Jesus tells a story about sheep and goats. He uses his remarkable parable to illustrate how God approaches humans – women and men – through other men and women.

The parable begins with Jesus explaining that when he returns *"in his glory"* to judge the world, he will separate out the *"sheep"* and *"goats."* The sheep will spend eternity with him while the goats will be sent to the *"eternal fire prepared for the devil and his angels."*

The big surprise is that the sheep don't recognize themselves as righteous and ask why they are being spared ("righteous" meaning just, morally right and, by implication, innocent and holy).

Jesus then says that the righteous, the sheep, are saved because they gave him food when he was hungry. They gave him drink when he was thirsty. They welcomed him when he came to them as a stranger. They clothed him when he was naked. They visited him when he was sick. And they came to him when he was in prison. The righteous are stunned. They ask, *"When did we do these things?"* Jesus responds that whatever they did for others, they did for him.

Years ago, I heard Dr. Anthony Campolo, a well-known educator, pastor and author, explain the parable this way: Every encounter with another human is an encounter with Jesus and an encounter with Jesus is an encounter with God. "People are not God," said Campolo. "People are not Jesus. But the God who died on the cross is a God who comes at us through people. If you can't love him in people, I contend that you can't love him."

In Matthew, Jesus is speaking to both the women and men among his disciples; nowhere in the parable does he distinguish between genders. Just as God may approach us through men or women in need, God asks women and men to respond out of love. And He never gives us something to do without also providing the tools we need to accomplish His will. Thus, equal access to serve comes with equal access to the tools required to serve.

Jesus instructs his followers about serving others

Matthew 20:20-28 – The mother of Zebedee's sons (the Apostles James and John) went to Jesus and asked that her sons be honored in his Kingdom with seats on the left and right of his throne. This angered the other apostles. Responding like the exceptional leader and communicator he was, *"Jesus called them together and said, 'You know that the rulers of the Gentiles lord it over them and their high officials exercise authority over them. Not so with you. Instead, whoever wants to become great among you must be your servant and whoever wants to be first must be your slave – just as the Son of Man did not come to be served, but to serve and to give his life as a ransom for many.'"*

As in the parable about sheep and goats, Jesus emphasizes that his followers are those who are willing to serve others, without regard to position, gender, wealth, race, education or any of the other ways we humans tend to divide ourselves.

In all the verses mentioned above (John 17, Matthew 25 and Matthew 20), Jesus is preparing the apostles to take his place as teachers and reconcilers when he returns to heaven.

If serving rather than being served is an overarching principle for his hand-picked team of apostles, how can we think it does not apply to all Christ followers, be they male or female, single or married? If Jesus wants us to serve one another, why are so many of us, like the mother of Zebedee's sons, concerned about issues of power and authority?

More references regarding Jesus and women disciples

John 4:39 – Women were not allowed to testify in the Jewish and Greco-Roman cultures, yet after Jesus spoke to the Samaritan woman this happened: *"Many Samaritans from that town believed in him [Jesus] because of the woman's testimony."*

John 20: 17-18 – Jesus appoints the first post-resurrection evangelist to testify on his behalf. Her testimony: *"'I have seen the Lord!' And she told them that he had said these things to her."* See also Matthew 28:9-10, Mark 16:7, 9-11, Luke 24:10.

Luke 8:1-3 – These verses talk about the people who traveled with Jesus. They include several women disciples.

Luke 10:38-42 – Jesus is at the home of Mary and Martha. Mary is praised for her eagerness to listen to the teaching of Jesus, rather than stay in the kitchen. You can't get the full impact of this Scripture without remembering the cultural and religious practices of the day. Rabbis did not teach women in or out of the synagogue, nor were women allowed to talk with men in public. Contact was even limited in their own homes. Mary's presence at the feet of Jesus wouldn't have upset only her sister Martha; her presence in a room full of men would have set them on edge, too.

Perhaps Mary got caught up in the moment and forgot her place, or maybe she was a woman of tremendous courage. Either way, Jesus says she is doing the right thing even though she is breaking all the rules of her day.

Jesus speaks about marriage, now and later

Matthew 19 – Jesus confirms that God is the originator of marriage between a man and a woman by pointing back to Genesis. He also confirms the seriousness of the marriage commitment, though he recognizes divorce as an unhappy possibility in a fallen world. *"'Haven't you read,' he replied, 'that at the beginning the Creator "made them male and female," and said, "For this reason a man will leave his father and mother and be united to his wife and the two will become one flesh"? So they are no longer two, but one flesh. Therefore what God has joined together, let no one separate.'"* (For the full quote, see Matthew 19:1-12.)

Matthew 22:29-33 – Speaking about marriage in the heavenly realm, Jesus tells a group of Pharisees: *"'You are in error because you do not know the Scriptures or the power of God. At the resurrection people will neither marry nor be given in marriage; they will be like the angels in heaven. But about the resurrection of the dead – have you not read what God said to you, 'I am the God of Abraham, the God of Isaac and the God of Jacob'? He is not the God of the dead but of the living. When the crowds heard this, they were astonished at his teaching."*

What the apostles taught after Jesus' resurrection

Acts 2:14-18 – This section of Scripture describes what happened on the day of Pentecost, when God's Holy Spirit was given to His people. This was not long after the resurrection of Jesus. The gifts of the Holy Spirit described in Acts are for men and women: *"Then Peter stood up with the eleven, raised his voice and addressed the crowd: 'Fellow Jews and all of you who live in Jerusalem, let me explain this to you; listen carefully to what I say. These people are not drunk, as you suppose. It's only nine in the morning! No, this is what* *was spoken by the prophet Joel: 'In the last days, God says, I will pour out my Spirit on all people. Your sons and daughters will prophesy, your young men will see visions, your old men will dream dreams. Even on my servants, both men and women, I will pour out my Spirit in those days and they will prophesy.'"*

Peter's words are notable for his inclusion of women. A first-century woman, hearing what he said, would quickly catch their significance. They and the men were being told that as followers of the Christ, women would receive the same spiritual gifts as men. And, in fact, women did become prophets, teachers, church leaders and evangelists, as can be seen in the verses that follow.

Acts 21:8-9 – Philip the evangelist had four unmarried daughters. All of them prophesied (meaning they presented inspired messages or divine revelations). From these verses, it appears that Philip's daughters devoted themselves to the work of teaching rather than becoming wives and mothers, which sets them apart from their culture.

Prophetic statements coming from four young, single women must have been astonishing. Philip was not an obscure character – quite the opposite. He is first mentioned in Acts 6 as a deacon of the church in Jerusalem. In Acts 8, Philip is serving as an evangelist in Samaria, preaching and performing miracles. On the road from Jerusalem to Gaza, Philip meets an Ethiopian eunuch (Acts 8:26). His encounter with the Ethiopian contains one of the few records in the New Testament of an individual's conversion to Christ follower.

The last time we see Philip is here in Acts 21, when Paul and his companions come to him for shelter. He is also visited by the prophets and elders of Jerusalem. Because Philip was well known among Christ followers, we can be sure his daughters were also well known.

Revelation 2:20-22 – This is an account of another woman prophet: *"Nevertheless, I have this against you: You tolerate that woman Jezebel, who calls herself a prophet. By her teaching, she misleads my servants into sexual immorality and the eating of food sacrificed to idols. I have given her time to repent of her immorality, but she is unwilling. So I will cast her on a bed of suffering."* Note that Jezebel is not condemned because she is a woman who teaches; the problem is wrong content.

How Paul's beliefs about women changed after his encounter with the risen Christ

Saul, who became known as Paul after he met Jesus, was a well-trained, up-and-coming leader among the Pharisees. He was educated by Gamaliel, one of the most famous teachers of his day, and Paul's dedication to Jewish values and traditions was beyond question. His commitment was such that he voluntarily became the leading persecutor of Christ followers as he sought to defend his God from what he considered to be a heretical new religion.

According to Paul's own account, after meeting Jesus on the road to Damascus (post resurrection) he became a different man, one who began to conform his life to that of Jesus. One change Paul must have made was to stop opening each new day with the traditional Jewish man's prayer that thanked God he wasn't born a Gentile, a slave or a woman. Selected by the risen Jesus to become an evangelist and teacher of the Christ followers he formerly sought to kill, Paul learned that a person's relationship with God is not dependent on race, social position, religious affiliation or gender; it begins with accepting Jesus as Messiah.

One of the more striking testimonies to Paul's new life as a Christ follower is seen in Acts 16. It is written by Luke, a Gentile physician who became a Christian through Paul and who traveled extensively with the apostle. Once again, credit goes to

Jake Hendrix for a sermon that pointed out the significance of the following event.

Luke tells us in Acts 16 that while Paul was on his second missionary journey he saw a vision of a man in Macedonia who was pleading for help. Paul's response was to immediately travel to that region with Silas and other companions. The capital of the province of Macedonia (northern Greece) was Philippi, a thriving Roman colony located on the edge of the Mediterranean Sea. It was there that Paul met Lydia, a prosperous business woman who dealt in purple cloth.

In those days, purple cloth was a valuable and expensive commodity usually worn as a sign of nobility or royalty. After listening to Paul's Gospel message, Lydia became the first person in Europe to accept Christ. She and her entire household were baptized. It is interesting to note that Lydia is also the first woman in the Bible to be identified by name when baptized, and these are not her only "firsts."

Luke tells us that after being baptized, Lydia persuaded Paul and his team to stay the night at her home. The result of their getting to know one another is that Lydia helped Paul found a church in Philippi – the first Christian church in all of Europe.

Everything about this brief account in Acts is remarkable:

- Paul's vision from God and his obedient response
- The former Pharisee sitting down to speak with a group of women who "just happened to be" ready to hear the Gospel
- Baptizing Lydia and her family
- Agreeing to stay the night in the home of a woman
- Working with Lydia and other women to found a church in Philippi

Keep in mind that Paul used to be a leader among the Pharisees, a man taught by the very best Jewish scholars. He persecuted Christians and believed it a sin to speak to a strange woman – let alone teach one – yet he accepted an invitation to Lydia's home and partnered with her to found a church.

There is no way in the world that Saul the Pharisee would have done what Paul the Christ follower did in Acts 16. This one example should be enough to convince the most reluctant readers that something significant caused Paul to reject the traditional male-dominant hierarchy that ruled his world (and still rules much of ours). And what was the result of this wildly improbable collaboration between Paul and Lydia? The church they founded brought the Gospel to Macedonia, thus opening the door to all of Europe.

Paul teaches about God's design for women and men

Do you still have doubts about Paul's understanding of how women are to function in this world? As the TV infomercials implore: Wait! There's more. The following paragraphs provide additional insights into what Paul learned from Jesus about God's design for male-female relationships.

I Corinthians 11: 8-9 – Woman was created *"for man."* The Greek preposition "dia" (for) never carries the thought of possession; it assigns cause or reason. Paul's meaning is that woman was created "on account of" man. Man was incomplete until Eve was created. She became Adam's companion, not his property. The generic human only became the individual man when the woman was created. Likewise, if God had created Eve first, humanity would have been incomplete without Adam. Both male and female are necessary to complete humanity, as per Genesis 1 and 2.

1 Corinthians 11:11-12 – *"Nevertheless, in the Lord woman is not independent of man, nor is man independent of woman. For as woman* *came from man, so also man is born of woman. But everything comes from God."* In verse 12, Paul uses the same word, "dia," in reference to man. He writes that man is *"born of"* (created for) woman, *"as woman came from"* (was created on account of) man. The source of man is woman's body and the source of woman is man's body. Paul is recognizing the God-created mutual dependency between men and women; he is not laying the groundwork for building a hierarchy.

2 Corinthians 5:14-21 – Christ died for all so that all can be reconciled to God and to one another. All means all; women and men, Jews and Gentiles.

Galatians 3:27-28 – Paul writes the following to the church at Galatia: *"For all of you who were baptized into Christ have clothed yourselves with Christ. There is neither Jew nor Gentile, neither slave nor free, nor is there male and female; for you are all one in Christ Jesus."* Here, Paul writes to believers that our spiritual unity in Christ is what binds us together and overcomes racial, social, gender or other boundaries that used to separate us.

Because we are united in Christ, there is no longer any spiritual difference between men and women, slaves and their masters or Jews and Greeks. Paul's words must have led to consternation in households that had slaves or that consisted of two Christian spouses. In homes where only one spouse was a believer, which was often the case, Paul's letter must have been dynamite.

Paul didn't want to blow up marriages or other male-female relationships. His goal was to bring understanding and order to newly forming church families, so that each member learned to follow the example set by Christ. His new teachings were difficult for the wider Jewish and Greco-Roman communities to accept, as they demonstrated by beating him, chasing him from town to town and imprisoning him on many occasions.

Keep Paul's new view of women in mind as you read other writings from him that appear, at first glance, to contradict his new Christ-centered approach to life. Paul was a very smart, well-educated man, personally chosen by Jesus to represent him on Earth. Paul was not one to contradict Jesus or his own words.

Working with – and for – one another

1 Corinthians 11:4-5 – Paul acknowledges that both men and women pray and prophesy in church. (There is more about these verses on following pages.)

1 Corinthians 12 – Paul speaks of the church as a united body of believers in which every member is equally gifted and indispensable. Unlike Judaism and other religions, women were not excluded from leading and teaching in the first-century Christian church.

Philippians 2:1-8 – How are we to serve one another? Just like Jesus did: *"Therefore if you have any encouragement from being united with Christ, if any comfort from his love, if any common sharing in the Spirit, if any tenderness and compassion, then make my joy complete by being like-minded, having the same love, being one in spirit and of one mind. Do nothing out of selfish ambition or vain conceit. Rather, in humility value others above yourselves, not looking to your own interests but each of you to the interests of others. In your relationships with one another, have the same mindset as Christ Jesus: Who, being in very nature God, did not consider equality with God something to be used to his own advantage; rather, he made himself nothing by taking the very nature of a servant, being made in human likeness. And being found in appearance as a man, he humbled himself by becoming obedient to death – even death on a cross!"*

Philippians 4:2-3 – Two female co-workers of Paul are having an issue with each other. Paul writes: *"I plead with Euodia and I plead with Syntyche to be of the same mind in the Lord. Yes and I ask you, my true companion, help these women since they have contended at*

*my side in the cause of the gospel, along with Clement and the rest of
my co-workers, whose names are in the book of life."* The Greek word
Paul uses to describe these women is "sunergos." It means "an
associate, helper or fellow worker." The same word describes
Clement, the man named in this passage.

1 Timothy 2:8-15 – Please see Chapter 5 for an in-depth
discussion of this portion of Paul's letter to Timothy and the
Christians in Ephesus

Women servant-leaders in the early church

Romans 16 – Paul names many women who were faithful in
ministry. Included in this list is Phoebe, who Paul calls a "sister."
It is interesting that Phoebe's name means "bright" or "luminous."
Names had meaning in Paul's time; bright seems to fit Phoebe
well, given her accomplishments as a Christ follower.

The Greek word Paul chooses to describe his sister in Christ
is "diakonos." Depending on the translation you read, Paul is
referring to Phoebe as a servant, helper, minister, deacon or
deaconess. "Diakonos" is the same word Paul uses to describe
his own ministry. Examples include: 1 Corinthians 3:5; 2
Corinthians 3:6, 6:4 and 11:23.

He also acknowledges that Phoebe's ministry is equally as
important and valid as that of other early church leaders such
as Tychicus (Ephesians 6:21), Epaphras (Colossians 1:7) and
Timothy (1 Timothy 4:6), all of whom he refers to as ministers
or servants (diakonos) – same as Phoebe.

The original Greek word is gender neutral. It means the same
for men and women and should be translated the same for both.
Writing in *Ministry*, an international journal for pastors, Darius
Jankiewicz reports: "The distinctly feminine form 'diakonissa'
(deaconess) did not appear until the fourth century."

Paul's use of "diakonos" was not an accident. Phoebe was an office holder in the church at Cenchreae and Paul affirmed her position of authority in her church.

Paul's words are shocking when we consider his background as an up-and-coming leader of the Pharisees. If his personal encounter with the risen Christ had not turned his world upside down, Paul could never have played a significant role in lifting women from their secondary religious, social and marital status. But he did meet Jesus and that changed everything.

The feminine noun "prostatis"

Romans 16:2 – Paul refers to Phoebe as a "benefactor" (or leader) of many. The Greek word is "prostatis," a feminine noun. It carries the sense of a woman set over others, who cares for them and uses her resources on their behalf (*Thayer's Greek Lexicon*). Most English translations refer to Phoebe as a "helper," even though the better translation is "leader."

Some have suggested that Paul's letter to the church in Rome was carried there by Phoebe. Perhaps the build-up he gives her in his letter to the Romans had to do, in part, with Paul's desire that Phoebe get a proper welcome once she got there. If she was his courier, Paul was asking her to do a job traditionally handled by men, just as Jesus asked Mary Magdalene to carry the news of his resurrection to his apostles.

Another passage that may refer to women as deacons is found in 1 Timothy 3:11. That text can be read two ways: as referring to women who are deacons or to wives of deacons.

Other women mentioned in Romans 16

16:3 – Priscilla is listed before her husband Aquila. This was unusual and may mean she was more involved in the early church than her husband. In Acts 18:26, Priscilla is again listed first, perhaps because she took the lead in completing the theological education of Apollos, a prominent and highly educated man. Paul refers to Priscilla and Aquila as his "co-laborers" or "companions in labor" (sunergos).

16:6 – Mary worked hard (kopiaó) for her brothers and sisters in faith. The same word describes good leaders in 1 Thessalonians 5:12. The word means to feel fatigue, be wearied.

16:7 – Junia is the subject of some debate, but is probably the wife of Andronicus. The two *"were in Christ"* before Paul was and he says they were outstanding missionaries (or apostles; those sent out). The Greek word translated as "outstanding" is "episemos," which means remarkable, eminent, of note.

16:12 – Tryphena and Tryphosa are probably sisters. They are identified as hard workers (kopiaó), like Mary. Persis (a Persian woman) also worked hard and was loved by Paul. The word he uses is "agapétos," meaning beloved, dear.

16:13 – Paul refers to the mother of Rufus as caring for him like his own mother.

16:14-15 – Julia, the sister of Nereus and other "sisters" are included in a list with males who, like them, are referred to as *"saints"* or *"the Lord's people."* The Greek word for saint is "hagios," meaning set apart by (or for) God, physically pure, morally blameless, holy.

Does Paul send a mixed message regarding the role of women?

In 1 Corinthians 1:10, Paul asks for all believers to set aside their differences and live in unity. In Ephesians 4:11-13, he calls for believers to use their gifts to build up the body of Christ so there is maturity and unity of faith.

There are many other New Testament calls to unity, but not one that encourages followers of Jesus to worry about who is in charge of whom. Our model is always Jesus, and his time on Earth showed that he valued service over power and position.

Even knowing what Jesus said and did while on Earth doesn't satisfy everyone, though, especially when the Bible contains Paul's seemingly contradictory statements about the roles of men and women. Is everyone equal, as indicated in 1 Corinthians 7, Romans 16 and Galatians 3 or is there a hierarchy, as some believe Paul is indicating in 1 Corinthians 11 and Ephesians 5?

I first learned of the great debate in mid-1970 and since then have spent many hours thinking about the scholarly arguments for both sides. My personal belief after more than 40 years of considering the topic is that the focus belongs on:

- How Jesus treated women

- How Paul would have treated women as a strict Pharisee versus how he spoke of them and worked with them when he became a Christ follower

- How we model the behavior of Jesus and Paul. The way they overturned the cultural roles of women serves as a valuable guide for us, even as we sometimes struggle to understand a few of Paul's writings

The only way Paul could possibly follow in the footsteps of Jesus was to first toss out the beliefs and traditions that defined him right up to the moment he met God in the flesh. That's when Paul became an apostle of Christ, instead of a persecutor of Christians.

Not long after, Paul began to work with and praise women of faith who served as church leaders; who served as teachers of men and women; and who in other ways ministered to the blossoming early church. Paul could never have commended these women if Jesus had not already begun to repair the relationships that the sin of Adam and Eve tore apart.

Early teething problems when women joined men in the church

1 Corinthians 14 – Paul deals with participants who are creating chaos at church gatherings in Corinth. Keep in mind that the New Testament always refers to the "church" as a community of believers, not a building. This definition is especially important when talking about male and female roles in church (meaning within the Christian community).

Some who believe women should not teach or preach inside church buildings have no problem with them teaching and preaching in homes or as missionaries working outside their own countries. This is inconsistent with the New Testament use of "church." If they can preach or teach anywhere, they can preach or teach everywhere.

Paul mentions several times that he is writing to his "brothers and sisters" at Corinth. While instructing them about gifts of the Spirit and how to have orderly church gatherings, he tells them, *"Since you are eager for gifts of the Spirit, try to excel in those that build up the church"* (verse 12). In verse 20, Paul continues to emphasize that he is writing to *"brothers and sisters."*

Then, in verses 26-33, while still teaching them how to be orderly in their meetings, he writes, *"What then shall we say, brothers and sisters? When you come together, each of you has a hymn, or a word of instruction, a revelation, a tongue or an interpretation. Everything must be done so that the church may be built up. If anyone speaks in a tongue, two – or at the most three – should speak, one at a time and someone must interpret. If there is no interpreter, the speaker should keep quiet in the church and speak to himself and to God. Two or three prophets should speak and the others should weigh carefully what is said. And if a revelation comes to someone who is sitting down, the first speaker should stop. For you can all prophesy in turn so that everyone may be instructed and encouraged. The spirits of prophets are subject to*

*the control of prophets. For God is not a God of disorder but of peace — as
in all the congregations of the Lord's people."*

These verses indicate that Paul expects women to participate
with the men. The problem he is addressing has to do with how
to remain orderly, so as to build up the church and not scare
away those who are new to the body of faith.

Paul calls for a certain type of silence ...
but it's not necessarily what we first think

In verses 34-40 of 1 Corinthians 14, Paul seems to take a quick
U-turn from what we've just read, when he writes this: *"Women
should remain silent in the churches. They are not allowed to speak,
but must be in submission, as the law says. If they want to inquire
about something, they should ask their own husbands at home; for it is
disgraceful for a woman to speak in the church. Or did the word of God
originate with you? Or are you the only people it has reached? If anyone
thinks they are a prophet or otherwise gifted by the Spirit, let them
acknowledge that what I am writing to you is the Lord's command. But if
anyone ignores this, they will themselves be ignored. Therefore, my brothers
and sisters, be eager to prophesy and do not forbid speaking in tongues.
But everything should be done in a fitting and orderly way."*

There is much to consider in this section of Scripture. Even
Paul's instruction that husbands and wives should talk about
issues of faith at home broke new ground in their culture.
Without a good Greek dictionary, it is difficult to make sense
out of these passages. Fortunately, even if you don't have a Greek
dictionary in your home library, some of the best reference books
are available for free on the web.

In this case, the dictionaries confirm that Paul has several
choices for words that indicate "speak." Each of the choices
conveys a significant difference. The word Paul chose for these
passages is "laleó," which here carries the connotation of "an
extended or random harangue." It's from the root "lalos,"

meaning talkative (*Strong's Exhaustive Concordance*). Paul is not telling women they can't speak or pray in church. He is telling them not to give long speeches or rants. He is writing about a particular way of speaking in church gatherings that was disruptive.

The women were new to faith and new to meeting with men. It is not surprising that things weren't going all that smoothly in Corinth. Every church gathering must have seemed like a new believers' church class that was being taught by new believers for new believers, many of whom had never been educated, let alone educated in theology.

At least some of the women must have overreacted to their new freedom. It is also likely that many of the men were not happy to welcome women into the church body as full participants. Obviously, when Paul wrote to his *"brothers and sisters"* in the Corinthian church, tension and chaos were issues. His words were intended to bring order to their gatherings.

In this light, Paul's letter makes perfect sense. Have you ever participated in a gathering of people that includes just one person who has never been in a group discussion before but is excited about sharing his or her thoughts and has a lot to say? It is not at all unusual for the newcomer to monopolize the conversation with questions and comments. Often, a leader has to take that person aside and gently let him or her know how to participate without dominating. That's what the apostle does in his letter, only it is not just one person who needs instruction, it is everyone.

I encourage you to compare Eugene Peterson's superb modern language translation of 1 Corinthians 14:33-40 in *The Message* to other translations. *The Message* says, in part: *"When we worship the right way, God doesn't stir us up into confusion; he brings us into harmony. This goes for all the churches — no exceptions. Wives must not disrupt worship, talking when they should be listening, asking questions that could more appropriately be asked of their husbands at home. God's Book of the law guides our manners and customs here. Wives have no license to use the time of worship for unwarranted speaking. Do you — both women and men — imagine that you're a sacred oracle determining what's right and wrong? Do you think everything revolves around you?"*

Regarding marriage and "headship"

1 Corinthians 7 — New Testament scholar Dr. S. Scott Bartchy points out that Paul gives equal time to men and women throughout Chapter 7 when he describes a mutuality in sexual relationships (7:2-5) and teaches that men and women are complete persons in Christ without marriage or children (7:7-9).

Dr. Bartchy is a first-century historian who has studied and written about male-female roles from a biblical perspective since the 1970's. A respected author of numerous books and essays on the subject, he is a retired UCLA professor and was the founding director of UCLA's Center for the Study of Religion.

In an essay titled, "*Some Theses about Gender Roles, Headship and Submission*," Dr. Bartchy writes that "Paul applies Jesus' definition of power as strength for serving others (See, e.g., Mark 10:35-45) … when he urges that the husband belongs to the wife in the very same way as the wife belongs to the husband (1 Corinthians 7:2-5); when he addresses both women and men regarding divorce (calling on Jesus' authority in 7:10-13); and when he notes that a Christian woman (as well as a Christian man) has the power to make 'clean' a marriage to a non-believer (7:14-16)."

Dr. Bartchy continues: "Paul also implicitly calls into question the authority of the oldest male family member by addressing Christian women without reference to their husbands' authority, as well as Christian slaves without reference to their owners." All of the above were radical social statements in a culture that thought women incapable of wisdom and believed that "a perfect virtue is absolutely unthinkable in women." (The quote is from Pseudo-Lucian, a Greek dialogue popular in ancient times and reflective of views about women in Paul's day.)

Power that is freely conferred

No man in the Jewish or Greco-Roman cultures of that time thought that women had the slightest ounce of authority over their husbands. They were, after all, the "property" of their men. Yet Paul tells the Corinthians that the *"wife does not have authority over her own body but yields it to her husband. In the same way, the husband does not have authority over his own body but yields it to his wife. Do not deprive each other except perhaps by mutual consent."* (1 Corinthians 7:4-5).

Dr. Bartchy points out that the word for authority Paul uses is "exousia," which is not the same word he chooses when speaking of man as the head of woman in 1 Corinthians 11 and Ephesians 5. Here, "exousia" refers to the authority husbands and wives give each other. "Exousia" is conferred or delegated power. When both give away their power, neither can be said to rule over the other.

1 Corinthians 11:1-3 – In Chapter 10, Paul tells the people of Corinth that his purpose in writing is to seek *"the good of many, so that they may be saved."* In Chapter 11 he encourages them, *"Follow my example, as I follow the example of Christ."* Paul's challenge is to bring peace and order to a chaotic church in Corinth, a church that is trying to follow a Christ who taught principles, not rules or regulations.

Jesus' principles were based on loving God and loving others. He never sought to force his authority on those who opposed him. He never discussed what it was like to be the instrument of creation. Jesus was zeroed in on teaching his followers how to love with all their hearts, minds and souls; how to love as servants, not rulers.

This being the case, what does Paul mean in 1 Corinthians 11:3, when he begins a section about prayer by telling the Corinthians that *"the head of every man is Christ and the head of the woman is man and the head of Christ is God."* This is a difficult passage; one that has led to countless debates, especially over the meaning of "kephalé," the Greek word that Paul uses for head.

Paul, a well-educated and precise writer, deliberately chooses "kephalé" over other options. As a result, prominent pastors and scholars of ancient languages and cultures have written thousands of words on the subject – and they still do not agree about the meaning of the verse. The common argument of those who insist that men are designed to serve as "heads" over women is that "kephalé" means "authority over," as in the ruling power of one who must be obeyed.

As the authorities over women, this view claims, men are the ultimate decision makers and leaders in a hierarchy that goes through them to Jesus and then to God. How this view is supposed to play out in homes, churches and workplaces for women who are married, unmarried and widowed is not explained in the New Testament and leads to a variety of other disagreements.

A second viewpoint is that "kephalé" did not mean authority or ruler in Paul's time; he chose "kephalé" for head because it meant the beginning or source of a thing's existence. Using "beginning" as the definition, verse 3 means that God is the source of Jesus, who is the source of man, who is the source of woman.

Most Greek lexicons favor an "authority over" definition for "kephalé." Many Bible scholars, however, believe that "beginning" or "source" fits better than "authority over," especially in the overall context of how Jesus and Paul welcomed women into their presence and into their ministries.

As happens all too often, a word, "kephalé," has been used to divide Christians into bickering camps of "complementarians" and "egalitarians." The former believe that men are designed to hold authority over women; the latter believe that God intends for all to hold equal status and equal roles. For the record, I detest this sort of labeling as, I believe, would Jesus and his apostles. Labels like "complementarian" and "egalitarian" create walls. Jesus intends that we remove the walls and unite around him, even though we sometimes disagree about the specifics of how to live out his commands.

Marriage and headship continued – "kephalé" revisited

Ephesians 5:17-24 – Paul encourages the church to be wise and to understand the will of God. Verse 21 continues the thought about living wisely with the exhortation to, *"Submit to one another out of reverence for Christ."* This is an overarching principle for what he is about to write. Dr. Bartchy calls this a "forceful application of Jesus' definition of power," where self-subordination to other Christians is presented as a characteristic of the Spirit-filled life.

In Ephesians 5:22-23, the "kephalé" argument comes up once again: *"Wives, submit yourselves to your own husbands as you do to the Lord. For the husband is the head of the wife as Christ is the head of the church, his body, of which he is the Savior."*

What did submit mean to Paul?

Let's consider the word "submit" before spending more time on "kephalé." Paul uses "hupotasso" in verses 21 and 22. It means to voluntarily yield out of love for someone else. (See also 1 Corinthians 16:16, 1 Peter 5:5 and Colossians 3:18 for similar uses of the word. Colossians 3:18-22, in fact, closely parallels

Ephesians 5 in regards to Paul's instructions to wives, husbands, children and slaves.)

His use of submission does not mean obedience required by law or when there is no other choice. In Ephesians 5, Paul speaks about submission or obedience in relation to four groups of people:

1. **5:21** - All Christ followers submit to one another (hupotasso).

2. **5:22 & 24** - Wives submit to husbands (hupotasso, implied in 24).

3. **6:1** - Children obey (hupakouó).

4. **6:5** - Slaves obey (hupakouó).

The latter two examples use "hupakouó" for "obey" and provide an important contrast to Paul's use of "hupotasso." "Hupakouó" means to obey a command or authority because there is no other choice, as a slave obeys a master, a subject obeys a king or a child obeys a parent. When it came to obeying an authority figure, slaves had no choice, nor did children.   Prior to Christ, women were in the same fix as slaves and children.

Women had been taught to be submissive to men, not just to their husbands and fathers. Submission, in fact, was necessary for their psychological and physical survival. Jesus brought a dramatic change in male-female relationships, as we've noted several times, and that change carried over to marriages.

The marriage of two Christ followers could no longer be about the husband holding power over his wife. Marriage was returned to its original design as a one-flesh partnership in which both husband and wife submit to each other (hupotasso), motivated by the same love (agapaó) that caused Christ to die on the cross for his Church. Dr. Bartchy explains that "agapaó" love carries the sense of doing what the Lord prefers, by His power and direction. Paul makes the appeal for husbands to exhibit "agapaó" love to their wives three times in Ephesians 5:25-33 and each time he is saying, in effect, "Men this isn't me talking, it is God instructing you through me."

Richard Foster writes about mutual submission in *Celebration of Discipline*: "In submission we are at last free to value other people. …We have entered into a new, wonderful, glorious freedom, the freedom to give up our own rights for the good of others." Foster's book puts into modern words the thought Paul wrote to the church in Corinth almost 2,000 years earlier: "*Though I am free and belong to no one, I have made myself a slave to everyone, to win as many as possible*" (1 Corinthians 9:19).

The submission Paul speaks of to both the Corinthians and Ephesians is meant to be voluntary and mutual. It is not one sided. Dr. Bartchy points out that one-sided submission "tends to produce children and parents, not adults. It inhibits Christ-centered autonomy in adult Christians and produces conformity and rebelliousness in Christian groups."

"Christians are urged to 'count others better' than themselves (Philippians 2:3-4) as the chief expression of sharing in the 'mind of Christ Jesus' (2:5)," writes Dr. Bartchy, "and to 'outdo one another in showing honor' to each other (Romans 12:10) as a demonstration of having 'transformed minds. (12:2).

"Submission is developed by God in a climate of acceptance, honesty and caring. It is not produced by people's efforts to pressure one another or to control the processes of love. Submission must come from God, be sustained by Him and be open to change by Him. Human beings want to control relationships; God wants to free them to develop and grow in love and mutual support."

Loving one another, submitting to one another and serving one another required massive changes in behavior for these first-century men and women. It requires the same of men and women today, especially those who have been focused on who's in control, instead of how to serve one another.

Submitting out of reverence for Christ

Jesus is the key to all human relationships, in or out of marriage. To revere this Christ, as Paul teaches in Ephesians 5:21, is to hold him in high esteem, to honor and respect him. Revering him and having loving feelings aren't enough, though. Jesus insists that we act on our love: *"If you love me, keep my commands"* (John 14:15).

What does this type of love look like in a husband-wife relationship? Consider, once again, how Jesus demonstrated his love. He gave up his position of authority – stooped down – to come into our physical world as a baby in an impoverished family. He grew into a man who lived to serve the humans he created.

Even though many people rejected him, he demonstrated how much we are loved by giving his life for us. It is to this Jesus that Christian men and women submit and willingly choose to serve. This is how husbands and wives are to love and serve one another.

Getting back to "kephalé" in Ephesians 5:23

To me, Paul's statement that *"the husband is the head of the wife as Christ is the head of the church"* is most consistent with everything else he writes if "kephalé" is read as "source or beginning."

Without Jesus, there is no church, thus, he is the beginning of the church as well as the ruler or authority over it. But even though Christ had the authority to rule while walking among us, he chose to serve. That's the important lesson, no matter which side one takes in the great "kephalé" debate.

Another reason I believe the "authority over" translation does not work is that Jesus never indicated by words or behavior that males are to rule over females, nor is there anything in Genesis 1 and 2 to indicate that males are to rule over females. What we have, instead, is the Genesis 3:16 prediction (or curse) that comes after the Fall. Thousands of years later it is still playing havoc with relationships.

Dr. Troy W. Martin is a professor of biblical studies at Xavier University. In a paper entitled, "*Performing the Head Role: Man is the Head of Woman*," Dr. Martin summarizes the argument that "kephalé" should be defined as "source" this way:

- "Kephalé" normally does not mean "ruler"

- The ancient world did not (universally) think the head controlled the body

- The Septuagint shows that "kephalé" can mean "source."

In his paper, Dr. Martin cites Dr. Wayne Grudem, who is one of the better-known advocates of the more traditional "authority over" argument. After long research into ancient Greek usage of "kephalé," Grudem wrote that he found 49 examples (out of some 2,300 uses of "kephalé") that meant "authority over." This led Grudem to conclude that the first two points above are not correct and the third is suspect. Grudem conceded that there may be examples of "kephalé" indicating "source," though he did not find any.

But Martin and others have found "source" examples and Martin notes some of them in his paper. One ancient text reads, "The heart is the source (kephalé) of blood; the head [is the source] of phlegm; the spleen [is the source] of water; and the region above the liver [is the source] of bile. These four are the sources of these [fluids]."

Another text he cites is *Aristotle's Problemata 867a23-27*: "Why does the face sweat most? Is it because sweat passes most easily through parts which are rare and moist? And the head seems to be the source (kephalé) of moisture, as it is due to the considerable moisture that the hair grows."

Martin notes that "kephalé" is used in the singular in these two examples, as it is in 1 Corinthians 11:3 and Ephesians 5:23. The word is understood to mean the source of something. "To these texts," Dr. Martin writes, "can be added others that present parts of the head as sources of something." His paper then gives further examples.

Does physiology play a role in defining kephalé?

Martin also points out that the ancients were still debating the physiological roles of head and heart. An early author such as Paul chose his words to reflect whether he thought the center of intellect was in the heart or head. Plato, Plutarch and Philo were three philosophers who believed the head was responsible for thinking and decision making. Aristotle and others thought that sound thinking came from the heart.

Martin explains that the Apostle Paul's thinking was in line with that of Aristotle, favoring the heart as the seat of intelligence and decision making. In Romans 1:21, Paul writes, *"For although they knew God, they neither glorified him as God nor gave thanks to him, but their thinking became futile and their foolish hearts were darkened."*

Likewise, in 1 Corinthians 2:9, 1 Corinthians 4:5 and 2 Corinthians 3:15, Paul indicates that the heart is the center of intellect. In every case, he uses the Greek word "kardia," which means the literal heart of a person, but which also is used to indicate thoughts or feelings (of the mind).

Given Paul's view of physiology, Martin concludes that if Paul wanted to identify man as the leader, controller or ruler of woman his metaphor would have said that man was the heart of woman. To say that man is her head and mean "authority over," he finds, is inconsistent with what is known about Paul.

Furthermore, he writes that Grudem's 49 ancient examples using "kephalé" to mean "authority over" are not relevant, because they all came from authors such as Plato, Philo and Plutarch who believed the head was the center of control in the body. That is the opposite of what Aristotle, Paul and others believed.

Keeping the focus on Jesus

Regardless of how we translate the difficult "kephalé" passages, the key question remains the same: How did Christ lead the church? And we know the answer. He led as a servant, not as a king. He led by example, not with force; lovingly, not with a sense of entitlement.

Jesus and his apostles treated women as intelligent, capable servants of the Living God. This was a remarkable culture shift and such change would not have come without difficulties.

Chapter 4 – Main points summarized

1. Jewish men were not the only ones who felt it their right to control women and who expected to be served by women. All across the world, cultures mirrored the same type of patriarchal structures. Where did this universal idea of male domination come from? Is it just because men tend to be bigger and stronger than the women they rule? No, it all goes back to Genesis 1-3, when God's original design was corrupted by sin.

2. The starting point for returning the world to God's original design was the coming of Jesus, the Messiah, as explained in Chapter 3 of this book. God's desire is always to repair what human moral failures tear apart.

3. Jesus, through whom the world was created, became a servant to his own creations. His willingness to step down into our world from his place of honor in the heavenly realm provides the best example for how God wants us to treat one another. We are to focus on service rather than being served.

4. Jesus' teachings and behavior were not guided by cultural rules and traditions. He rejected the cultural practices of the first century by welcoming women into his group of disciples (learners), talking with them, showing them respect and giving them key roles in spreading his message. Because we know that Jesus came to reconcile all of creation to God, we can also trust that the rules and traditions he changed were contrary to God's original design for humanity.

5. Jesus taught both women and men to love God, love one another, unite around him and his Father and serve one another as he served them.

6. Jesus' famous sheep and goats parable (Matthew 25) shows that both women and men will be judged according to how we

demonstrate our love for our fellow humans. We are to use actions, not just words or kind thoughts.

7. Matthew 20 presents an overarching principle for all Christ followers. Jesus taught his apostles that those who wished to be first in his kingdom were to serve others as he did, without regard to gender, race or any other factor. Christ followers in this world may be granted power and authority, but regardless of our personal status, following him always requires serving others as he served.

8. John 4 and John 20 both contain examples of Jesus speaking to women who then testify on his behalf to other men and women. This is in direct conflict with the culture of the day that did not allow women to give testimony on behalf of (or against) a man or speak to men in public settings.

9. Jesus speaks about marriage in Matthew 19 and 22, giving credence to the accuracy of Genesis 1 and 2, confirming that Adam and Eve were real humans and tying God's original design for men and women to his own teachings.

10. Acts 2 describes the day of Pentecost, when Peter spoke about the gifts of the Holy Spirit being given to women and men. Acts 21 tells that four unmarried women used their gifts to advance the Gospel.

11. Saul was a rising star among the Pharisees and committed to stamping out the new "heresy" taught by Jesus. Then he encountered the risen Lord. That changed everything for Saul, including his name, which became Paul. The new apostle quickly learned from Jesus that a person's relationship with God no longer depended on birth, gender or religious affiliation; it is based on accepting Jesus as Lord. Acts 16 and the account of Lydia affirm that instead of being served by women, the former Pharisee worked alongside Lydia and other women to spread the Gospel. The result of collaborating with Lydia in Philippi is that

all of Europe was opened to the Gospel. Paul's rejection of the traditional Jewish view of women's roles is hugely significant.

12. Translations of 1 Corinthians 11, typically have Paul writing that woman was created "for man." The original Greek transcript shows his meaning to be that woman was created "on account of" man. Paul also wrote that as woman is created for man, man is created for woman. They are created for each other. Paul was showing that there is a mutual dependency between men and women.

13. Galatians 3 says: *"For all of you who were baptized into Christ have clothed yourselves with Christ. There is neither Jew nor Gentile, neither slave nor free, nor is there male and female; for you are all one in Christ Jesus."* Paul writes to believers that our spiritual unity in Christ transcends racial, social and gender boundaries.

14. In Paul's letters to various individuals and churches, he strives to bring order to new groups of male and female Christ followers who are struggling to come together for the first time. 1 Corinthians 12 recognizes that all members are gifted and indispensable to the community of faith. Philippians 2 explains that we are to learn how to serve one another by looking at how Jesus served us. In Romans 16, Paul names a number of women who were instrumental in the ministries of the early church, including Phoebe, who served as an elected or appointed leader in Cenchreae.

15. Paul calls for unity when writing to Corinth and asks believers in Ephesus to use their gifts to build up the church. 1 Corinthians 7, Romans 16 and Galatians 3 indicate that men and women are equally gifted to serve the church. I Corinthians 11 and Galatians 5 appear to limit women in some aspects of church life. To work through my thoughts on these Scriptures, I considered how Jesus treated women, how Paul would have treated them if he were still a law-keeping Pharisee and how

Paul actually did work with women after becoming a follower of Jesus. Paul could not have followed Jesus without first rejecting his old cultural and religious traditions regarding women. Something changed him. According to Paul, that "something" was his encounter with Jesus.

16. 1 Corinthians 14 deals with a church in chaos as it tries to welcome women into male-only gatherings for the first time, reconcile the teachings of Jesus with Judaism and exist in a culture that saw the early church as rebellious and potentially dangerous. The goal of Paul's letter was to bring order from the chaos, all the while making it clear he expected women to participate with the men.

17. Passages in 1 Corinthians 14:34-40 have long been used to keep women from church leadership roles. When Paul uses the Greek word "laleó," however, he is not contradicting his other instructions by telling women never to speak in church. He is telling them not to rant or give long speeches. He is seeking to bring order to people who are not used to meeting together and who have been given few guidelines for how to behave in their new Christ-centered community gatherings. Eugene Peterson's *The Message* provides a superb modern translation of these important verses.

18. Regarding 1 Corinthians 7, Scott Bartchy writes that "Paul applies Jesus' definition of power as strength for serving others." The Apostle also describes a mutuality in sexual relationships between married couples. He says that husbands belong to wives just as wives belong to husbands and, in Christ, the old male hierarchy becomes a thing of the past. (See, for instance, 1 Corinthians 7:4-5.)

19. Bartchy writes that in 1 Corinthians 11 and Ephesians 5, Paul uses the Greek word "exousia" to mean "authority." Paul's use

of "exousia" indicates that men and women are to freely grant power to one another. When both men and women freely give away their power, neither can be said to rule over the other.

20. 1 Corinthians 11:3 brings up the debate over the meaning of "kephalé," the Greek word used to indicate head. "Kephalé" can mean either "authority over" or "source of," and the word has long divided people of faith. Did Paul write that women are under the "headship" of husbands, fathers, or sons, as the Pharisees believed, or was he referring to the unity implied by the fact that God is the beginning, or source, of both men and women?

21. In Ephesians 5:21, Paul writes that all Christ followers are to submit to one another. These words are usually overshadowed by verses 22-23, which tell wives to submit to their husbands. The Greek word Paul chooses for submit is "hupotasso," which means to voluntarily yield out of love for someone else. The same word is implied in verse 24 and used in 1 Corinthians 16:16 and 1 Peter 5:5. In Ephesians 6:1 and 6:5, children and slaves are also told to submit, but Paul uses a different Greek word, "hupakouó." This time slaves and children are told to obey because they are under the authority of someone else. Paul's uses of "hupotasso" and "hupakouó" show the contrast between voluntary submission and the submission one gives when there is no choice. Paul is telling his readers that the marriage of two Christ followers is no longer about the husband holding power over his wife. Marriage is a partnership, motivated by love.

22. When Paul uses "kephalé" in Ephesians 5 to write that "the husband is the head of the wife as Christ is the head of the church," some read this to mean "authority over" and others read it to mean "source of." Ask yourself if the "authority over" translation corresponds with how Jesus and Paul treated women. Did they rule over them as traditional men ruled over their

women or did they introduce a new model for how men are to treat the women in their lives?

23. Dr. Troy W. Martin writes that his research refutes that of Dr. Wayne Grudem, a leading advocate of the "authority over" argument. Dr. Martin found a significant number of examples in ancient texts that use "kephalé" to mean "source" or "beginning." He also writes that the ancients were still debating the physiological roles of head and heart when Paul was alive. At the time the church was born, authors based their writing on how they viewed the role of head and heart. Paul viewed the heart as the seat of intelligence and decision making, as per Romans 1:21, 1 Corinthians 2:9 and 4:5 and other verses. Given Paul's view of head versus heart, Dr. Martin concludes that Paul's language in the Scriptures is not consistent with a view that man is meant to be the authority over women.

24. The key to understanding how God wants men and women to interact is seen in Jesus. He willingly gave up his place in God's world to come into our world as a servant. How he spoke with, taught and gave ministry assignments to women clearly demonstrated that the traditional Jewish views about the roles of women no longer applied to his followers. Then there was Paul, the hand-picked apostle of Jesus. We who live in the 21st century may disagree about how Paul meant us to understand words such as "kephalé" and "hupotasso," but it is hard to ignore that both Jesus and Paul turned traditional male-female roles completely upside down in the first days of the Church. There is simply no way Paul could have maintained his traditional Pharisaical views of women and still worked side by side with them to further the work of the Gospel.

Chapter 5

Key Thought:

This look at 1 Timothy 2:8-15 digs into a controversial section of Scripture that is used to explain why many churches prohibit women from serving as leaders and teachers of men. I did not plan to cover these verses in a separate chapter. However, after spending hours pondering the variety of scholarly explanations now available, I felt it important to offer enough information so you can decide for yourself what Paul wanted Christ followers to learn from his words. As a friend often says in matters like this, "Keep your mind open, but not so open your brains fall out."

1 Timothy 2:8-15

Therefore I want the men everywhere to pray, lifting up holy hands without anger or disputing. 9 I also want the women to dress modestly, with decency and propriety, adorning themselves, not with elaborate hairstyles or gold or pearls or expensive clothes, 10 but with good deeds, appropriate for women who profess to worship God. 11 A woman should learn in quietness and full submission. 12 I do not permit a woman to teach or to assume authority over a man; she must be quiet. 13 For Adam was formed first, then Eve. 14 And Adam was not the one deceived; it was the woman who was deceived and became a sinner.

15 But women will be saved through childbearing — if they continue in faith, love and holiness with propriety.

Timothy was a young pastor in Ephesus, which is located in present-day Turkey. He was well known to the Apostle Paul as a friend and co-worker on Paul's missionary journeys. Paul's letter to Timothy contains words of encouragement. Paul also provides instructions for the young pastor and the Christ followers he is ministering to in Ephesus.

The main subjects in this letter are false doctrines and orderly worship. That's what Paul tells us at the beginning of his letter and that's what he reaffirms in the final paragraph (1 Timothy 6:20-21).

Important background about Ephesus and the city's goddess

Roughly 120 years before Jesus was born, the Romans took control of Ephesus and made it the capital of their province of Asia. As a Roman capital city, Ephesus was a center of power and prestige. Its residents lived in the Roman Empire's wealthiest province and were known as a diverse, cultured mix of people who enjoyed the arts, music, dancing and a luxurious lifestyle.

The city was first settled largely by Greek colonists and later became home to a considerable number of Jews. Ephesus also was home to the huge, ornate Temple of Artemis. This famous and influential goddess of Greek mythology was known by the Romans as Diana. She was said to be the daughter of Zeus and Leto, and twin sister of Apollo.

The temple was destroyed and rebuilt several times. An ancient Roman historian wrote that the largest and most grand version was 425 feet long by 220 feet wide and had 127 60-foot-tall marble pillars. This is about twice the size of the Greek Parthenon in Athens. The temple was such an amazing architectural achievement that it became known as one of the Seven Wonders of the Ancient World. The temple brought a great many Artemis worshipers to Ephesus. This constant stream of visitors fed lucrative businesses that were geared to tourism and the selling of portable shrines. Thus, Artemis was important both religiously and commercially to Ephesus.

Dr. Sandra Glahn, a prolific author and an associate professor in Media Arts and Worship at Dallas Theological Seminary, writes about the effect of modern historical discoveries and technology in an essay titled, "The Identity of Artemis In First-Century Ephesus" (*DTS Magazine*, July 15, 2015).

She says, "In addition to the unearthing of ancient sites and to expanding social history explorations, one more development is worth noting. Today thousands of inscriptions from the first centuries B.C. and A.D. have been unearthed and become easily accessible via an online, searchable concordance." The benefit, she writes, is that scholars from around the world can do their research and share their findings much more easily than before.

What researchers have found is that Artemis was not worshiped the same in Ephesus as in other parts of the ancient world. For hundreds of years, her story appears to have evolved as the Ephesians added new myths and incorporated bits and pieces once attributed to other deities. Syncretism, the mixing of belief systems (in this case the mixing of beliefs about various gods and goddesses), was as popular in ancient times as it is in our "enlightened" post-modern age. As a result, Artemis looked different and had different roles as one traveled throughout the world.

It is widely agreed that in Paul's day, Artemis of Ephesus (also referred to as "Artemis Ephesia") was seen as the city's guardian; a strong, easily offended goddess with the power to determine who would live or die.

Dr. Glahn writes that the name Artemis means, "To be safe and sound." Glahn also provides several references that link Artemis Ephesia with childbearing and "midwifery." These include Plutarch, in his biography of Alexander the Great; an orator and poet named Zonas; and an author named Strabo who lived during the same century as Paul.

Scholars frequently describe the goddess as "mother Artemis," "a nurturing mother of everything," and as a ruthless "goddess of the hunt." They also link Artemis worship with animal sacrifices, temple prostitution and other sexual practices. Glahn presents a different view. She says her current research shows that the goddess was not personally "associated with sex, fertility or nurturing," though Artemis was believed to have the ability to protect a woman during childbirth.

According to tradition, the city of Ephesus was founded by Amazon warrior women. The first Ephesian shrine to Artemis was believed to have been created by Otrera, a goddess known as the first Amazon Queen. Otrera was said to be either the wife or daughter of the war-god Ares. Whether real warrior women played a role in founding Ephesus or not, the city's citizens believed it was true and they believed that Artemis and the city's female founders were more than a match for any man.

One legend claimed, "Amazon procreation was confined to an annual event with a neighboring tribe. Baby boys were sent back to their fathers, while the girls were trained to become warriors" (Amanda Foreman, "The Amazon Women: Is There Any Truth Behind the Myth?" *Smithsonian Magazine*, April 2014).

Some scholars have written that the Temple of Artemis was a female-only cult, but that does not now appear to be the case. While women had a significant role in Artemis worship, there were both priests and priestesses.

The *International Standard Bible Encyclopedia's* entry for "Diana; Artemis," published in 1915, says temple prostitution was involved. Glahn's newer research leans in the opposite direction, toward an emphasis on asceticism practiced by "eunuchs and virgins."

While scholars may disagree about specific beliefs and practices associated with Artemis and the Ephesians, it is impossible to ignore the influence this goddess had on the people who worshiped her before they met Jesus.

Paul's travels to Ephesus

Ephesus was more of a paternal society by the time Paul and Timothy arrived on the scene, but Artemis was still viewed as the city's goddess-mother-protector. Because childbirth was the number one cause of death for Ephesian women, it must have been very hard for new Christ followers to let go of the protections they believed Artemis provided, especially her protection during birth. (Keep this in mind when we consider 1 Timothy 2:15.)

Paul's first visit to Ephesus is chronicled beginning in Acts 18. He stopped there to preach while on his second missionary journey, in about 51 A.D. Paul was urged to stay in Ephesus by those who wanted to learn more about Christ. Instead, he chose to move on to Jerusalem.

In about 54 A.D., as seen in 1 Corinthians 15:31-32, Paul refers to fighting *"wild beasts"* in Ephesus (metaphorical beasts). A few verses later, in 16:7-9, he says he wants to return to Ephesus because, *"a great door for effective work has opened to me and there are many who oppose me."*

According to Glahn, Homer once wrote about Artemis, referring to her as a "queen of all wild beasts." (Homer is the name given to a famous Greek poet who wrote in 850 B.C.)

Paul's 1 Corinthians reference, therefore, may indicate he knew Ephesian history. He most certainly knew enough about the current culture to expect a great deal of resistance should he make a return trip to that city. But even with *"wild beasts"* awaiting him, the apostle was still determined to walk through the door that God *"opened to me."*

In Acts 19, we learn that Paul's second visit to Ephesus came in about 54-57 A.D., during his third missionary journey. During the nearly three years he stayed there, his preaching caused so many Ephesians to turn away from Artemis and the occult that those who made a living off of such things saw Paul as a threat to their economic success. They eventually rioted against him.

While trying to calm a violent crowd that wanted to tear into Paul, the city clerk of Ephesus gave further testimony as to the significance of Artemis: *"Fellow Ephesians, doesn't all the world know that the city of Ephesus is the guardian of the temple of the great Artemis and of her image, which fell from heaven?"* (Acts 9:35).

After Paul left the city for the second time, he sent a message asking the Ephesian elders to join him in a nearby town, away from the hostility he had just escaped.

There, he again spoke of Ephesus in colorful terms: *"Keep watch over yourselves and all the flock of which the Holy Spirit has made you overseers. Be shepherds of the church of God, which he bought with his own blood. I know that after I leave, savage wolves will come in among you and will not spare the flock. Even from your own number men will arise and distort the truth in order to draw away disciples after them. So be on your guard! Remember that for three years I never stopped warning each of you night and day with tears"* (Acts 20:28-31).

God prevails, even in hostile environments

Acts is generally thought to have been written between 60 and 65 A.D., in the same window of time as Paul's Ephesian letter.

What is said about Paul in Acts and what he writes in Ephesians are well worth reading before considering 1 Timothy, which also fits into this same time period (about 64 A.D.).

The dates tell us that more than a decade after Paul's first visit to Ephesus, the church was still struggling with false doctrines, there was still disorder during times of worship and the city's *"wild beasts"* and *"savage wolves"* were still resisting Christ.

As opposition to Christianity becomes increasingly vocal in our current world, I find it inspiring to read that the church of Paul's day continued to grow despite severe, often violent, opposition. This is a good reminder that God is never defeated by a hostile environment, nor does He abandon His people who live in the midst of such situations.

Looking inside the Ephesian church

The church was composed of men and women, slaves and free, Jews and Gentiles, educated and uneducated, rich and poor. This mixed group of new believers did not make it easy on church leaders as they tried to develop a united family of faith in the midst of a hostile culture.

Well-known Christians who played key roles in Ephesus included the Apostle John, Priscilla, Aquila, Apollos and, of course, Timothy. Tradition says that Mary, the mother of Jesus, also lived in Ephesus toward the end of her life and that both she and John are buried there.

Prior to becoming Christ followers, many members of the new church would not have socialized or worshiped together. Think of the uniqueness of what was happening. Rather than worshiping Jehovah or pagan gods in separate temples, Jews and Gentiles were breaking bread together as they worshiped Jesus.

Women were joining the men as if they belonged. The poor were sitting next to their rich superiors like equals. Slaves were acting as free as those who owned them. Add in that these new Christ followers were bringing their old beliefs and traditions into the church and it is easy to see why it was such a challenge to develop unity among the faithful.

To put this in a modern context, imagine that a new prophet comes to Orthodox Islam in the heart of Saudi Arabia. This prophet allows women to worship with the men and Shiite and Sunni to meet together. In fact, this prophet welcomes to worship all men and women who were once considered infidels. After bringing these earthshaking changes to Islam, the prophet tells them to love one another and then goes away without leaving specific guidelines for how the mixed bunch is to work this out, in worship or otherwise.

Can you picture the result? There would be theological arguments, confusion and anger inside the church, not to mention more of the same directed at them by outside religious leaders and the government. This is just the sort of chaos Paul writes about.

It is sad that by addressing false doctrines and how to keep peace in worship gatherings, Paul's words give rise to a divisive, centuries-long debate about women's roles in the church. There are several main camps. One argues that in the second chapter of his first letter to Timothy, Paul prohibits women from teaching or holding authority over men everywhere and for all time. Likewise, in worship settings then and now, men are to do the speaking while women remain silent learners.

Another group argues that Paul's instructions about men leading women are meant for all time, but women may speak in worship services if under the authority of a man. A third view says that Paul's words don't mean what the others think they do. Paul was writing to correct a heresy (or heresies) being taught in Ephesus. He was not presenting a universal rule that men must lead and women follow, nor was he excluding women from speaking during community worship times.

Points to ponder

Before we look at these controversial verses, please consider the following:

1. New Testament instructions about "church" and communal worship refer to gatherings of Christians; "church" is never a building. It logically follows that biblical rules about who can teach and lead in church must apply to all such gatherings, not just those in certain buildings owned or used by specific church communities.

2. Paul was a strict, rules-keeping Pharisee until he became a follower of Jesus. Christians first came to know him by how he ruthlessly pursued them.

3. Paul's view of God and how to serve Him changed dramatically after he became a follower of Jesus. As a result, the same people Paul tried to murder learned to trust him with their lives.

To see how much Paul changed after meeting the risen Jesus, all we have to do is compare Saul the Pharisee with Paul the Christ follower. When looking at specific verses in 1 Timothy, it is important to remember the broader context of his letter. Who is Paul writing to? What is going on? What response does Paul expect his words to generate?

Paul's letter – which reveals only one-half of a two-way conversation with Timothy – is preserved in the Bible so that generations of Christ followers can learn from him. Are we meant to benefit from seeing how Paul treated a specific situation at a specific point in time or was Paul's objective to produce a general epistle that contained rules the worldwide church would live with forever?

Addressing community worship

We know that Paul's letter gives Timothy advice on how to mold his unruly flock into a harmonious church family. Doctrinal errors are a major part of the problem. Paul writes in his letter that he is planning to return to Ephesus for a third visit but isn't sure it will happen: *"Although I hope to come to you soon, I am writing you these instructions so that, if I am delayed, you will know how people ought to conduct themselves in God's household"* (1 Timothy 3:14-15).

The first chapter of Paul's letter to Timothy begins by addressing the topic in general. His second chapter gets more specific, with instructions about community worship and prayer. Verses 2:1-7 discuss who to pray for and are tied to verse 2:8 by "therefore." This means that the following verses are still about prayer, but now the topic is how to pray.

Verse 8 speaks to a prayer and worship problem the men were having. To link the thought in verse 8 to what he is saying in the next two, Paul uses the Greek word "hosautos" ("likewise" or "I also want"). Next, he begins to speak directly to the women (bypassing their husbands).

Both men and women were participating in worship inappropriately, so Paul explains how he wants both to behave. Men were arguing with one another to the point of anger and this is hardly a fitting prelude to corporate prayer and worship. Women were placing more emphasis on personal appearance and status than their worship of God. Like the men, they were not in a proper frame of mind to approach their Creator in prayer.

Paul tells the men and women to calm down. To the women, he adds that they are to clothe themselves with *"good deeds, appropriate for women who profess to worship God."* In other words, stop trying to impress one another with how you dress and what

you own. Let your actions demonstrate who you are as followers
of Jesus.

Apparently, some of the women were from an elite upper
class and were flaunting their wealth. They may have expected
deference from men and women of lesser standing. Perhaps they
were also inclined to assume authority in a gathering of other
believers who were not of their elevated social standing.

Examining some of Paul's most disputed words

Verses 11-12 are where serious controversy begins. Eugene
Peterson translates them this way in *The Message:* *"I don't let
women take over and tell the men what to do. They should study to be
quiet and obedient along with everyone else."*

Were the women of Ephesus abusing their new-found freedom
in Christ? Were at least some of the women aggressively taking
over church gatherings, despite not knowing much about their
new faith? Were wealth and status factors? Were practices
learned in the Temple of Artemis influencing how the Ephesians
followed Christ?

All of the above seem likely, especially when we observe how
common it still is for men and women to carry cultural and
religious beliefs and practices from one setting to another.

Is Paul speed-shifting from local to global concerns?

Many teachers and scholars believe that Paul is shifting gears
rather abruptly in verse 11, moving from how to pray in the
Ephesian church into a discussion of male-female roles in the
global church. They use this and following verses to reinforce
the view that Paul's words form a universal prohibition against
women teaching and leading in the church.

This view, it seems to me, is the same as claiming that God
does not want men to learn about Him from women and may

infer that even an incompetent man is a more able leader than a competent woman. Such views fly in the face of God's original design as seen in Genesis 1-3, bear no resemblance to what Jesus taught and demonstrated and are completely at odds with what Paul taught and demonstrated.

There is also a view that says verse 11 refers to one woman in particular who was sowing discord with her false teachings. This is because the verse can be translated, *"Let the woman learn in silence."* The NIV translation is, *"A woman should learn,"* and the Revised Standard Version (RSV) is, *"Let a woman learn."* It seems more likely that numerous people were involved. Paul's letters have already told us that false doctrines and other church issues had plagued the Ephesian Christians for more than a decade by the time Paul wrote to Timothy.

A rocky beginning for a new tradition

It is often overlooked that Paul – like Jesus – taught women about faith matters right along with the men. The letter to Timothy is a major departure from tradition in that: (1) Both women and men are being instructed on how to behave in common gatherings and (2) Paul bypasses their husbands (or other male authorities) to teach the women directly.

In Chapter 3 of this book we saw that Jesus welcomed women into his band of followers and specifically chose individual women to testify on his behalf to both men and women; we saw how he spoke with women privately (outside the presence of a husband or other male authority); and we saw that Jesus answered questions from both male and female disciples in mixed settings.

As for Paul, in other letters he commends women for teaching men and for leading in their churches. One of the most striking examples is the time Paul spent with Lydia and other women to form the first church in Europe. Lydia was no shrinking violet, nor was Priscilla, who the Ephesians most certainly knew played a leading role in the education of Apollos. Priscilla and Apollos both lived in Ephesus and participated in that church.

When the church gathered together, is it likely Paul required these highly capable women to sit in silence while only men were free to share prayers and teachings? Does this sound like the same Paul who in 1 Corinthians 11:2-6 tells women how to pray and prophesy in their community worship services? Or the Paul who explains in Colossians 3:16 how men and women are to conduct themselves during their times of worship together? Or the Paul of Romans 16, who commends an entire list of women for their service to the church?

Furthermore, the view that women can't speak, lead or teach men about matters of faith in "church" is inconsistent unless it includes home communities, the mission field, the writing of books and lesson plans and even – it would seem – church-run schools and seminaries.

Another inconsistency is that some churches limit women in their home churches, but allow them to teach Christ to men in foreign countries. There is also a tacit agreement among many Christian groups that women can teach young men up to a certain age, but not after. The New Testament says nothing about how to determine when a boy becomes a man.

Do these inconsistent, even contradictory, traditions really come from Paul and Jesus or from our own misunderstandings of biblical teachings?

One woman's perspective

Sherry Bradley is a friend my wife, Raelene, and I met in a Sunday Bible class about 40 years ago. When I asked her and other friends for their take on Paul's words to Timothy, Sherry wrote the following insightful paragraphs: "When I step back and look at the 'bigger picture,' I know that Jesus' birth and death changed everything. Females were elevated to a position not known before. Their souls became equal with men … and that was, I think, the problem at that point in time … that Paul addressed the issue of 'false teachings' and perhaps the women (with their new-found freedom) took things too far. I believe that because of specific issues and situations in that church, Paul had to rein things in tightly.

"The sharply worded instructions in verses 9-15 are given for the purpose of getting women's attention – and quickly. Each time I read them, they bring me up straight … and cause me to reflect on my attitude in worship. The best learning experiences I have had as a Christian occur when I am quiet, listen to God speaking to me and submit myself to what he wants me to learn."

Taking a closer look at verse 11

A literal translation of verse 11 is that women should learn in "quietness" and "submission." According to *Strong's Concordance*, the Greek word for "quietness" is "hésuchia," which refers to a "God-produced calm which includes an inner tranquility that supports appropriate action. This term does not mean speechlessness, which is more directly indicated by the Greek word 'sige.'"

I believe Paul is instructing the women and men in Ephesus to quiet themselves and develop a calm inner state that is conducive to both worship and learning. He uses "hésuchia" instead of "sige" because he does not intend that women sit in church like silent statues from his day forward.

Dr. Gail Wallace, an adjunct professor at Azusa Pacific University, points out that "hésuchia" is the same word used in 2 Thessalonians 3:12, where Paul instructs people to *"settle down,"* and in 1 Timothy 2:2, where he tells the church to pray *"for kings and all those in authority, that we may live peaceful and quiet lives."*

Her conclusion is, "It does not seem Paul's intention [in verse 11] was that women would never speak at all." Many disagree with that conclusion. Christian author Bobby Valentine wants to know why. How, he asks, can people believe "hésuchia" in verse 11 restricts women for all time, but "hésuchia" in the two citations just noted does not command Paul's male disciples to lives of silent worship?

Yet another inconsistency is the argument that because Jesus never selected any women to join his inner circle of apostles, he never intended them to lead or teach in his church. The problem with this is that Jesus also failed to select any Gentiles to his inner circle. This did not prevent Jesus from later commissioning Paul as a missionary to the Gentiles, and then commissioning Gentile leaders through Paul. Nor did it prevent Luke, a Gentile, from writing his Gospel.

The Bible contains many examples of Gentiles in leadership positions in the early church. It would be foolish to suggest that Gentiles should be prohibited from teaching or serving as missionaries because Jesus never named any as apostles. It seems equally as wrong to use the same argument to prohibit women from exercising their gifts of teaching and leadership.

Submitting to further analysis

Now that we've looked at the meaning of "quietness," it's time to define "submission." Paul uses the Greek noun "hupotage" in verse 11. "Hupotage" is derived from "hupotasso." In his other letters, Paul uses "hupotasso" to express the general principle that men and women are to submit willingly to one another out of love, both in church and at home. He uses "hupakouó" when there is no choice about submitting to authority, as discussed in the previous chapter.

In 2 Corinthians 9:13, where Paul writes of the "obedience that accompanies your confession of the gospel of Christ," he is referring to willing submission (hupotage). In Galatians 2:5, he writes that he did not place himself in subjection (hupotage) to false teachers for even a moment. Paul is referring to the fact that he did not willingly submit.

Paul speaks about leadership in families and churches when he provides qualifications for church leaders in 1 Timothy 3:4. He writes that a deacon must *"manage his own family well and see that his children obey (submit to) him."* Again Paul uses "hupotage," willing submission. As a side note, I don't believe Paul is writing that deacons must be parents. He's saying a deacon who is a parent must demonstrate the ability to lovingly guide his or her children toward willing submission. Paul is not looking for authoritarian deacons whose children submit only because they have no other choice. That doesn't bode well for their children or for how such deacons would lead at church.

Paul knew that managing well does not include ruling a household (or church) by sheer force of will. Jesus was a loving servant-leader. His style is the model for all who seek to lead in Christian communities.

While on the topic, it is worth noting that although Paul requires a high standard for church leaders, it is a rare parent who never faces times when a child refuses to willingly submit to his or her authority (the teen years come quickly to mind). If Paul meant for these rebellious times to rule us out of church leadership, few parents could ever qualify. It is also true that those who are well-qualified to be church leaders may sometimes need to focus their time on issues in their own families rather than on the broader church family.

Paul writes more about submission in Titus 2:5, when he encourages wives to willingly submit to their husbands (hupotage). And in Titus 2:9, he exhorts Christian slaves to be obedient to their masters. Slaves were already in forced subservience. Now Paul is encouraging them to adopt an attitude of willing submission (see Ephesians 6).

Paul does not endorse slavery. As in many of Paul's letters, being unchained spiritually does not mean his followers are immediately freed from physical bondage. He recognizes that the standards of the world are often at war with Christ. To quote N.T. Wright, "You simply can't take a community all the way from where it currently is to where you would ideally like it to be in a single flying leap."

Paul can, however, insist that followers of Jesus immediately begin to treat one another as much-loved brothers and sisters, knowing that this heart change will lead to improved lives for everyone, especially those currently bound by unjust laws and traditions.

In summary, I believe 1 Timothy 2:11 continues Paul's teaching about how to behave in a gathering of the church family. His use of "hupotage" reinforces the idea that Paul wants the women of Ephesus who are unqualified as teachers to willingly submit to both God and those who are qualified to teach them.

"I do not permit"

The NIV translation of 1 Timothy 2:12 is: *"I do not permit a woman to teach or to assume authority over a man; she must be quiet."* Does Paul's use of *"I do not permit"* (which can also be translated, *"I am not allowing"* or *"I am not now permitting"*) mean he is giving an instruction that applies to all churches for all time?

The word for "teach" in verse 12 is "didaskein." According to *Strong's*, it "nearly always refers to teaching the Scriptures." If Paul meant to institute a lifelong universal ban on women teaching biblical truth to men or serving as leaders within church communities, he contradicted himself every time he publicly commended them for teaching and leading. I find it hard to believe that Jesus would personally choose a double-minded fool to serve him. The better response to verse 12, I believe, is found when we think about other possible meanings of Paul's words to Timothy and the Ephesians.

When Paul wanted the Corinthian church to know that an instruction came directly from God, he wrote: *"For I received from the Lord what I also passed on to you"* (1 Corinthians 11:23).

When he wanted that same church to know that he was the originator of a different instruction, he wrote: *"To the rest I say this – I, not the Lord"* (1 Corinthians 7:12). In 1 Corinthians 7:25, Paul again distinguishes his personal practice from a regulation handed down by Jesus: *"I have no command from the Lord, but I give a judgment as one who by the Lord's mercy is trustworthy."*

Though I wish Paul had been more specific in his letter to Timothy, it is fair to assume that the people on both ends of this written dialogue knew one another so well there was no need to spell things out in great detail.

My belief is that Timothy and the church understood *"I do not permit"* as the shorthand equivalent of: "Jesus did not leave us a detailed guide for how to bring a diverse mix of people together to worship, so to keep our gatherings from getting too chaotic and uncomfortable for newcomers this is what I do." In other words, Paul's instructions were tailored to Ephesus; they were not intended to restrict the ministries of women for all time. But, as noted, this is me speaking, not the Lord.

Assuming authority?

"Assume authority" is another interesting phrase. It is from the seldom used Greek word "authentein." While "authentein" is found in ancient documents, verse 12 is the only time it appears in the New Testament. Paul most certainly had a specific point in mind when he chose it. The word can mean to have authority

over someone or something; connote an aggressive abuse of authority; or refer to literal or figurative violence (including murder).

In general, "authentein" is used to emphasize an authority that dominates. *Thayer's Greek-English Lexicon of the New Testament* says the word means: (1) One who with his own hands kills another or himself, (2) one who acts on his own authority, autocratic, (3) an absolute master and (4) to govern, exercise dominion over. *Strong's Exhaustive Concordance* says it means: "To act of oneself, i.e. (figuratively) dominate – usurp authority over."

Comparing "exousia," "proistemi," and "authentein"

Think back to the discussion of 1 Corinthians 7:4-5 in chapter 4. There, Paul told husbands and wives they do not have authority over their own bodies. He used "exousia," a word for authority that means spouses are to willingly delegate their power to one another. Paul selects "exousia" a number of times in other letters to speak of authority that is either freely given or freely withheld (1 Corinthians 6:12 and 9:4-6 are examples of the latter).

He uses another word for authority, "proistemi," when writing to Timothy (Chapters 3:4-5, 3:12 and 5:17). "Proistemi" carries the sense of one who has the kind of character and established reputation to lead or influence others effectively.

But here in 1 Timothy 2:12, Paul uses "authentein," which gives a third meaning. One way to translate *"I do not permit a woman ... to assume authority [authentein] over a man"* is this: *"I do not permit a woman (or women) to grab authority from a man (or men)."*

It seems likely that Paul used "authentein" because at least one woman – most likely more – aggressively claimed an authority to teach (an absolute mastery over others) that was creating problems.

Rev. Arnold J. Voigt, in his article, "Theses on Women in the Church," in the fall 1999 edition of *The Daystar Journal*, makes the case that, "The context suggests Paul is addressing wives and husbands, not just men and women in general. … The usages of 'aner' and 'gune' in this passage can well be translated 'husbands' and 'wives' instead of 'men' and 'women.'"

Voigt compares the uses of 'aner' and 'gune' in 1 Corinthians 14:34-36, 1 Peter 3:1-7, 1 Timothy 2:9-15 and other passages. He then writes, "Only two passages are not that absolutely clear, the two verses in our text: 'I desire that the man should pray …' and 'I do not permit a woman to teach or to govern a man.' Only these two passages seem ambiguous. Shall we then be absolutely dogmatic in insisting that these two instances must refer to males in general and not to husbands?"

Voigt's view is that the emphasis of these passages is on the behavior of Christian wives: "Wives were not to dominate or contradict husbands publicly and go against cultural custom." I leave it for you to decide if Paul was writing to husbands and wives or men and women in general.

Does Paul commend those who ignore his instructions?

When Paul's letters commend specific women for teaching men, he is making it clear that the Holy Spirit is not bound by culture or tradition. In 1 Corinthians 10:23 Paul says, *"I have the right to do anything,' you say — but not everything is beneficial. 'I have the right to do anything'— but not everything is constructive."* His words here and in 1 Corinthians 6:12 remind us there are times when we need to set our rights and/or traditions aside in order to accomplish something that is more important.

In my view, it is reasonable to say that Paul is applying this principle in Ephesus, as he does in Corinth. He may be teaching the church that even though the women in Ephesus have the right to certain ministries it is not beneficial that they insist on exercising all of their rights at this point in time. Their lack of doctrinal understanding and the circumstances of their cultural setting require that they quietly (not silently) soak in the lessons offered by Timothy and others who are qualified to teach them.

What we know for sure is that Paul's worship guidelines were meant to bring order to the church, because he tells us so. It is also likely that Paul wasn't just thinking of how the church functioned, but of the impression the church made on those who were looking in from the outside.

Christianity had already affected the businesses of those who sold their goods to worshipers of Artemis. Now Christians were messing with three other foundational pieces of their society: Artemis worship itself, male dominion over women (or female dominion over men) and the ownership of slaves. It is probable that Paul wanted to prevent an even larger backlash than Christians were already receiving from civil authorities, religious leaders and others (such as non-Christian men with Christian wives and slave owners with Christian slaves).

The first-century reality is that few women were qualified to lead their churches or to teach men. Most had not been educated as well as the men and their culture did not expect or want them to lead men, except, perhaps, in certain aspects of pagan worship. Furthermore, a man in their culture was likely to be shamed for allowing a woman to teach or lead him. Considering this, it is all the more impressive to read of the humility shown by Apollos, a man of high standing who welcomed the instruction of Priscilla.

Verses 13-15: Back to Genesis yet again

Paul's references to Genesis are cause for more debate. He writes in 1 Timothy 2:13: *"For Adam was formed first, then Eve."* Verse 14 states that Adam was not the one deceived; it was Eve who became the sinner. Verse 15 concludes this passage by saying that women will be saved through or in childbearing if they continue in faith.

What do these verses mean? Let's begin by looking at Paul's reminders that Adam was formed first and Eve was the first to sin. There are at least two ways to interpret these statements. One is with the male headship view, which claims that Adam was created first and, as such, was meant to lead. Eve came along later to serve as his helper. Those holding this view say that Adam made a serious mistake by allowing Eve to "incorrectly" take the lead when tempted by the serpent. They believe Paul is presenting this Genesis reference as a parallel to the dysfunction in Ephesus where women assumed leadership over men. Verse 15 is said to reinforce the idea that men are created to lead and women to stay home and raise families.

This interpretation of Paul's words breaks down on several levels, but especially as we remember that Genesis 3:6 says Adam was *"with her"* as Eve listened to Satan's arguments. To me, this shows that Adam was every bit as weak as Eve when it came to resisting temptation. Adam stood by in silence, watched his wife make a bad choice and then followed her off the same cliff.

If Adam was not deceived, as some believe Paul is indicating, he chose to sin willingly. Which is worse, to sin having been deceived or to sin on purpose? Or does it really make a difference? We know that God accepted no excuses or finger pointing from either Adam or Eve. He punished both.

Many continue to insist that God designed Adam with a stronger character than Eve's. This made him the natural leader and her the natural follower. As one who interviewed, hired and directed management-level men and women during a long business career, I see in Adam's behavior none of the qualities one looks for in a leader. For Paul to point back to Genesis 3 as a justification for placing men as leaders over women is mind-boggling. Paul was too smart, too experienced and too well educated to make such an error.

To understand verses 13-15, think about Paul's words in the context of his entire letter, including what we know about the religious, civil and social factors that influenced every aspect of life in Ephesus.

Dr. Rick Talbott, author of a book titled, *Jesus, Paul and Power: Rhetoric, Ritual and Metaphor in Ancient Mediterranean Christianity*, writes that Jesus and Paul lived in "a culture that was structurally, functionally and ideologically different from our modern Western culture to the degree that we cannot glibly impose our cultural assumptions on the texts."

As an example, he points out that the ancient world mixed religion and politics to a far greater degree than we can possibly imagine happening in our Western culture, where we tend to emphasize "a personal, introspective approach to religion."

Talbott's book is a reminder that Paul knew not to ignore how significant Artemis and the other gods and goddesses were to new Gentile Christians in Ephesus. Paul also knew that Jews came to Christ as monotheists, worshiping a God who *"is the same yesterday and today and forever"*(Hebrews 13:8). Paul had to find a way to unite a church full of people with wildly opposing views of God, even as some sought to custom-tailor Christ and Jehovah to suit Ephesian tastes.

Margaret Mowczko adds Gnosticism to the list of false doctrines that Paul was dealing with. She holds a Master of Arts degree in early Christian and Jewish studies. In her essay titled, "*1 Timothy 2:12 in Context*," she writes that early church leaders Tertullian (c. 160-220 A.D.) and Irenaeus (c. 130-202 A.D.) both identified Gnosticism as an issue in the first century Ephesian church. "Gnostics," she explains, "believe that it is special knowledge that brings salvation; however, this knowledge is secret, esoteric and only accessible to the few who can achieve transcendence."

It was hard for the Ephesians to give up their love of Artemis, the occult and other forms of special knowledge – the mysteries Paul writes about. This is reflected in Paul's Ephesian letter, where he speaks of the importance of Christ over and over and writes several times about the "mystery" of Christ being revealed. Paul tells the Ephesians in language they were used to that the revelation of Christ is available to all and supersedes all previous mysteries, obviously including those of Artemis, the occult and various forms of Gnosticism.

Christ's kingdom, Paul writes, is *"far above all rule and authority, power and dominion and every name that is invoked, not only in the present age but also in the one to come"*(Ephesians 1:21). And he warns the Ephesians about mixing the Gospel with *"empty words"* and *"fruitless deeds of darkness"*(Ephesians 5:6-11).

It is only about three years after the Ephesian letter that Paul writes to Timothy and a church still wrestling with false doctrines. In 1 Timothy 2:5, he says, *"For there is one God and one mediator between God and mankind, the man Christ Jesus."* He is making the point that there is no room for Artemis or any other old beliefs and practices in a gathering of Christ followers.

When I consider verse 5 with verses 13-15, I wonder if former Artemis worshipers were glorifying Eve at the expense of Christ, as they had once glorified their savior goddess? Did they conflate Eve with Artemis and see Eve as a protector and giver of life? Did they mistakenly believe it was Eve, as an Artemis-like goddess, who brought Adam into the world? Did they intend Eve to be the new "mediator?"

This is not mere speculation. Mowczko writes, "There were several Gnostic creation accounts which gave Eve primacy over Adam. In a few accounts, Eve was regarded as the first human being and, in some Gnostic texts, even as a member of the Godhead. She is sometimes referred to as 'the daughter of light,' 'the creator of the Logos,' 'the virgin,' and even specifically as 'the mother of Jesus.' In ancient Gnosticism, it was Eve who gave life to Adam. Moreover, Eve was a heroine to the Gnostics because she desired knowledge (gnosis) (Gen. 3:6)."

As Mowczko points out, Paul closes 1 Timothy with a final warning concerning a serious, Gnostic-like heresy: *"O Timothy, guard what has been entrusted to you, avoiding profane chatter and* **the opposing arguments of what is falsely called knowledge,** *which some have professed and thus gone astray from the faith. Grace be with you"* (1 Timothy 6:20-21, NASB, emphasis added).

The fog is clearing; we're marching toward a conclusion

Is it possible that we who struggle with verses 13-15 are making them more difficult than they ought to be? After considering Paul's words from every angle, after reading various histories of Artemis and Ephesus and after reading dozens of opinions from very smart people with widely varying viewpoints, an explanation began to emerge from the fog of information.

This explanation starts with Artemis. Paul's choice of words in his Ephesian letter and in 1 Timothy, tell us that worshipers of Artemis and other false gods and goddesses were bringing past beliefs and practices with them when they came to Christ. They were customizing the Gospel to suit Ephesus, just as they had created their own Ephesian version of Artemis.

It seems likely that Paul mentions Adam and Eve in his letter because at least some Ephesians found it difficult to give up the prestige of their powerful female goddess for a crucified male savior. Paul reminds the Ephesians that God is their creator. He first formed Adam and then created Eve. All other humans came from this beginning. Artemis didn't create anyone.

If the Ephesians were, in effect, creating a new goddess by transferring the power and prestige of Artemis to Eve, then verses 13-15 bring them back to reality. Eve could not have been an Artemis-style giver of life to Adam because, as Paul reminds them, Eve was formed after him. Not only that, she was the first to sin.

Paul doesn't write that Adam was *"not the one deceived"* to let Adam off the hook. God did not excuse Adam's sin, so Paul could not. Both Adam and Eve knew that eating from the tree of the knowledge of good and evil was forbidden. I believe Paul's message to the Ephesian church is that both Adam and Eve were human and not to be mixed into false doctrines about mythical gods and goddesses. By this, Paul showed that neither Eve nor Adam was worthy of worship. Neither could stand as a mediator between the Ephesians and the one true God. That role belongs exclusively to Christ. This teaching was directed to Ephesus, but it stands as a warning to all today who still insist on mixing other religious beliefs with the Gospel.

Paul's first letter to the Corinthians also places Adam in proper perspective to Jesus. In that letter, written about 10 years before the one to Timothy, Paul refers to the first Adam as an *"earthly man,"* contrasting him with Christ, who is *"of heaven."* In 1 Corinthians 15:22, Paul writes: *"For as in Adam all die, so in Christ all will be made alive."* When he writes that God has put everything *"under Christ"* (verse 27), Paul is emphasizing the clear distinction between the "earthly" first Adam who brought death to the Earth and the risen Christ who brings life.

To make sure the Corinthians don't miss his point, Paul adds in verses 45-47: *"So it is written: 'The first man Adam became a living being;' the last Adam [Christ], a life-giving spirit. The spiritual did not come first, but the natural and after that the spiritual. The first man was of the dust of the earth; the second man is of heaven."*

By contrasting the "natural" Adam who rebelled against God with the "spiritual" Adam who came to set things right, Paul not only clarifies the roles of Christ and Adam but rules out any confusion over whether Adam – or anyone other than Christ – was to be worshiped.

What Paul taught the Corinthians was surely shared with the Ephesians during his long stay in their city. In both Corinth and Ephesus, however, it seems that those who claimed to follow Jesus had a propensity for letting their eyes drift off of Christ and fasten onto false gods and false teachers. Good thing that doesn't happen to us now (he says with tongue firmly in cheek).

Stamping out false doctrines, not women teachers

Regarding 1 Timothy 2:14 and its relation to false teachings, Dr. Gail Wallace writes that Paul's words "probably sent the signal that by taking the role of teachers (and possibly in what they taught) these women had been deceived by heretics. It also implies that this activity was sinful."

"Probably" is too kind. In typical blunt fashion, Paul writes that there are false teachers in Ephesus who *do not know what they are talking about* (1 Timothy 1:7). Certainly, some of the women were deceived by these false teachers, just as Adam and Eve were deceived by the serpent.

This creates a situation that is similar to the one found in Revelation 2:20-22, where Jezebel is condemned for teaching false doctrines, but not for teaching. The sin in Ephesus is not that women are teaching men. It's that they jumped into teaching before they understood the Gospel and now are spreading false doctrines that lead people away from Christ.

Childbirth and salvation

I like Eugene Peterson's translation of 1 Timothy 2:15 in *The Message*: *"Adam was made first, then Eve; woman was deceived first – our pioneer in sin! — with Adam right on her heels. On the other hand, her childbearing brought about salvation, reversing Eve. But this salvation only comes to those who continue in faith, love and holiness, gathering it all into maturity. You can depend on this."*

Verse 15 tells us, in effect, that salvation comes through Eve because her descendant, Mary, gave birth to Jesus. By this, Eve reverses her sin and brings salvation to those who remain faithful to Christ.

Our friend Sherry Bradley writes: "In terms of childbirth, everything changed when Jesus was born. He came to take all of our sin upon himself and that included what happened with Adam and Eve. A woman birthed Jesus. Women (and men) are saved through their belief in Jesus, who came into this world through Mary. Childbirth is then the means for hope and grace and joy. For those of us females who have been able to give birth, we have shared in that wonder and been blessed by it. Since many women cannot conceive, I don't believe they are left out of salvation and certainly they aren't in a different classification. So, I think that verse 15 means that all women will be saved through Mary's childbearing of Jesus, the Savior."

Marriage, celibacy and salvation

Margaret Mowczko offers another perspective to this much-discussed verse. She believes that because Paul wanted the women of Ephesus "to know that getting married, having sex and having children ... would not jeopardize their salvation, as some ascetics taught ... Paul cleverly associates having children with moral purity and self-restraint. He does this because some people within the Ephesian church were forbidding marriage and teaching that celibacy was a necessary virtue (1 Timothy 4:3)."

Mowczko also points out that in 1 Timothy 5, "Paul encourages young widows to get married and have children, which they couldn't do if they held to the ascetic ideal of virginity and celibacy." By this teaching, she says, Paul is correcting "Gnostic extremes" that ranged from celibacy to "licentiousness." This view is similar to that of Sarah Sumner, Ph.D., in her excellent book, *Men andWomen In The Church*, which covers 1 Timothy in great detail.

Some also theorize that Paul was writing to counter a belief that because of Eve's sin, childbirth was a punishment to women that caused them to die while giving birth. N.T. Wright answers that theory this way: "Paul doesn't see it (childbirth) as a punishment. Rather, he offers an assurance that, though childbirth is indeed difficult, painful and dangerous, often the most testing moment in a woman's life, this is not a curse which must be taken as a sign of God's displeasure. God's salvation is promised to all, women and men, who follow Jesus in faith, love, holiness and prudence" (*"Women's Service in the Church: The Biblical Basis,"* by Dr. N.T. Wright, St. John's College, Durham, Sept. 4, 2004).

All of these explanations make sense in view of Paul's stated reasons for writing to Timothy, but there are even more ways to read verse 15. While staring at various translations for several weeks (figuratively and, at times, literally), I was reminded of a famous painting known as, "The Handkerchief of St. Veronica."

In 1874, German artist Gabriel Max caused a sensation with his painting of the face of Christ. What makes his art so special is that Max created an illusion; the eyes of Jesus can appear either open or closed. If you look into his eyes long enough, you will see them both ways.

I know because we have a reproduction from the 1920s that maintains the illusion. Some of our guests take a quick glance and only see his eyes open, or closed, but not both. Others look until they see Jesus' eyes change from open to closed or closed to open.

The painting serves as a metaphor for what happened to me. As I stared at 1 Timothy 2:15, I could see that Paul was making a connection between Eve giving birth, the arrival of Christ and salvation. The same connection is seen in Genesis 3:15 and 3:20. And then something clicked and I saw the verse in a whole new light. This is not to say that the explanations offered by others are wrong and I'm right. That's as inappropriate as insisting that Jesus' eyes in the Max painting are closed when a friend sees them as open. This is not a matter of making a verse say what we want it to. It is a recognition that well written prose often can be read on more than one level.

I believe that is the case with verse 15. I find many of the interpretations discussed in this chapter meaningful, yet there is another way to read the verse that hides in plain sight. Two common translations of the verse are: *"But women will be saved through childbearing"* (NIV) and, *"Notwithstanding she shall be saved in childbearing"*(KJV). My aha moment was to realize that the verse can be read: *"But women will be saved (kept safe) through (during) childbearing."*

For centuries Ephesians prayed to Artemis to protect women as they gave birth. As noted earlier, deaths during childbirth were so frequent it must have been difficult for new Christ followers to give up the protection of Artemis. I believe Paul is telling them that Eve doesn't replace Artemis; they are to place their faith in the true God – Jehovah – the one deity who is real, whose love is real and who has promised to keep them safe throughout eternity.

Here's how I arrive at this reading of verse 15: "Dia" is the preposition translated as "through" or "in." As discussed in Chapter 4 of this book, "dia" can assign cause or reason, or indicate the channel of an act (as per *The NAS New Testament Greek Lexicon*). In Chapter 4, we saw that examples of cause or reason include 1 Corinthians 11: 8-9 (woman was created *"for man"*) and 1 Corinthians 11:11-12 (*"man is born of"* woman). In these verses, Paul explains that God created mutual dependency between men and women. We are created for each other. To the people of Paul's day, this was a new idea.

The Bible does not teach that after Eve became the first to sin she was saved for childbirth – specifically saved to bring new lives into the world. If God hadn't saved both the man and the woman, life on Earth would look like DC Comic's *Dinosaur Island* or Steven Spielberg's *Jurassic Park*, without the human interlopers.

If it is not reasonable to suggest that women are saved primarily so they can continue giving birth and the Gospel doesn't teach that women are saved by giving birth, there must be at least one other option.

"Dia" as the channel of an act

One possibility is to read "dia" as the channel of an act. I've highlighted where "dia" is so used in the following examples. Acts 1:3 reads: *"After he had suffered, he had shown himself alive to them by many convincing proofs, appearing to them **during** a period of 40 days"* (International Standard Version, ISV). The NIV translation gives the same meaning: *"He appeared to them **over** a period of forty days."* Acts 5:19 reads: *"But **during** the night an angel of the Lord opened the doors of the jail"* (NIV).

If "dia" means "during" in 1 Timothy 2:15, the verse says that it is Jehovah, not another god or goddess, who keeps women safe during childbirth, *"if they continue in faith, love and holiness with propriety."*

What the verse does not explain is why women who follow the one true God still die in childbirth, as did those who prayed to Artemis. That would require a discussion of two different concepts: "safe" in our world and "safe" in God's world. The first is temporary; we're all going to die to this life at some point. The second refers to our choice as to whether we spend eternity with our loving Heavenly Father or outside the circle of His love.

It is my belief that Paul was cleaning up specific false doctrines that plagued Ephesus. He was not answering all of the theological questions that might have occurred to the men and women in Ephesus.

After reading this section of Scripture, my wife, Raelene, said she felt as if Paul was telling the women of Ephesus that they had "stumbled onto an important truth about their gender." She could hear Paul saying, "You do have a special place in creation and there is a god who values and protects you, but the god who honors womanhood is Jehovah, not Artemis."

The changes that came with accepting Christ reshaped how the women saw themselves religiously, politically and socially. In the past, as Talbott points out in his book, the honor ascribed to women was assigned at birth and was relatively fixed by their "inherited ethnicity, gender, wealth and family status."

Because of Christ, women were being offered new value as humans made in the image of God – with new power, new religious position and new social position. It is no surprise that working out these new concepts created friction with the men and led to confusion as to how to live in their reshaped world.

To learn more about the effects of shame and honor in Paul's ancient Mediterranean culture and how both defined male and female roles, check out Talbott's book, *Jesus, Paul and Power,* which includes a foreword by Dr. S. Scott Bartchy.

Are the eyes open or closed? Do verses 8-15 provide the answer?

Thinking back to the Gabriel Max painting of Jesus once again, whether the art shows our Lord's eyes open or closed depends on one's personal perspective. And, as we all know, serious Bible students and the scholars who teach them often see different meanings in Paul's words. I believe that what I see in these verses is what Paul wanted Timothy and the Ephesians to see. Others disagree.

What is impossible to dispute is that both Jesus and Paul welcomed women into their communities of Christ followers and commended their participation. Jesus and Paul not only allowed women to join the men as learners, they gave women roles as evangelists who spread the Gospel to both men and women. How then, I wonder, has this difficult-to-interpret portion of 1 Timothy become, for some, a definitive proof text that prohibits women from using their God-given gifts to lead and teach both men and women?

We live in a world that is often rocked by thoughts that go no deeper than a brief tweet or a late-night TV comic's wisecrack, so the following words of Gail Wallace provide a fitting close to this chapter: "Easy answers that either impose culture on God's will or neglect culture altogether must be resisted."

My additional caveat is that resisting easy answers is only a prelude. The rest of the journey involves digging into God's Word on our own; becoming "self-feeders" who not only study and pray over our Bibles, but who can discuss our beliefs in ways that encourage others to want to hear what we have to say.

A little bit of encouragement goes a long way

Decades ago, Scott Bartchy concluded a seminar on male-female roles by asking those of us in attendance: "Do not these [New Testament Scriptures] clearly suggest that Christians in the 20th century who want to behave as 'the people of God' should encourage girls and boys, men and women to discover their gifts in the Spirit (including gifts of leadership) and to devote them to the Body of Christ and its ministries?"

That question motivated my wife and me to begin our own study of what the Bible teaches about male-female roles. If you haven't already done your own research, I hope this book encourages you in the same way that Bartchy and others have encouraged us. Please, let this book become a starting point, not the end of the journey.

Therefore, I urge you, brothers and sisters, in view of God's mercy, to offer your bodies as a living sacrifice, holy and pleasing to God – this is your true and proper worship. Do not conform to the pattern of this world, but be transformed by the renewing of your mind. Then you will be able to test and approve what God's will is – his good, pleasing and perfect will. – Romans 12:1-2

Let the message of Christ dwell among you richly as you teach and admonish one another with all wisdom through psalms, hymns, and songs from the Spirit, singing to God with gratitude in your hearts.
                                                        – Colossians 3:16

For the word of God is alive and active. Sharper than any double-edged sword, it penetrates even to dividing soul and spirit, joints and marrow; it judges the thoughts and attitudes of the heart. Nothing in all creation is hidden from God's sight. Everything is uncovered and laid bare before the eyes of him to whom we must give account. Therefore, since we have a great high priest who has ascended into heaven, Jesus the Son of God, let us hold firmly to the faith we profess. For we do not have a high priest who is unable to empathize with our weaknesses, but we have one who has been tempted in every way, just as we are – yet he did not sin. Let us then approach God's throne of grace with confidence, so that we may receive mercy and find grace to help us in our time of need.
                                                        – Hebrews 4:12-16

Chapter 5 – Main Points Summarized

1. 1 Timothy 2:8-15 is often used to support prohibitions against women leading and/or teaching men in church communities. This section of Scripture is difficult to understand but too important to ignore.

2. The Apostle Paul is writing to Timothy and the church in Ephesus about false teaching and chaos in their gatherings.

3. Ephesus was a Roman capital city and a major center of influence throughout Asia Minor. The culture of the city was hugely affected by the worship of Artemis, a goddess connected to Ephesus for centuries prior to the birth of Jesus. Artemis was thought to be a strong, easily offended protector of the city, with the power to determine who would live or die and the ability to protect women during childbirth (the most frequent cause of death at that time). The Temple of Artemis was a "wonder of the world," causing tourists to flock to Ephesus to see it and worship there. This means Artemis was both religiously and economically significant to the city.

4. The following dates are approximate: Paul first visits Ephesus in 51 A.D. (Acts 18). In 54 A.D., he writes about that city in 1 Corinthians 15:31-32. His second visit to Ephesus (54-57 A.D.) is mentioned in Acts 19. In 61 A.D., Paul writes his Ephesian letter. About three years later, Paul follows with his letter to Timothy, who Paul left to guide the church in that city. As a result of these accounts, we know that the Ephesian church had been struggling with false doctrines and chaotic services for at least a decade when Paul wrote 1 Timothy.

5. The Ephesian church was a diverse mix of Jews, Greeks, Romans, slaves and free, men and women, rich and poor. Many came to Jesus having been worshipers of Artemis. Their culture

was accustomed to mixing religious beliefs and to creating their own versions of existing gods and goddesses.

6.   Paul says in his letter that he is addressing false doctrines being taught in that church and the unruly nature of their gatherings (1 Timothy, Chapters 1 and 3). At least some of their problems were related to Artemis worship.

7.   Verse 8 speaks to prayer and worship issues involving men, while verses 9 and 10 speak to problems the women were having. A major concern when reading these verses is Paul's intent. Is he speaking about specific problems in Ephesus and presenting solutions for Ephesus, or is he beginning with Ephesus and then abruptly transitioning into the presentation of a universal law that prohibits women from teaching or leading men for all time?

8.   Still considering verses 8-10, Paul tells the men and women that it is inappropriate to come to God in prayer and worship when they are arguing and angry with one another, when some are flaunting their wealth and social position and when at least some women had assumed teaching or leadership positions they are not qualified to hold. Paul tells the men and women to calm down; approach worship in a proper frame of mind.

9.   It is in verses 11 and 12 that the serious debate begins over the meaning of Paul's words. Is he telling unqualified women teachers – those teaching false doctrines – they need to become students or is he setting a permanent rule that prohibits women from leading and teaching whenever a Christian community gathers? The latter interpretation is in serious conflict with how Jesus and Paul welcomed women into formerly all-male gatherings and encouraged them to be disciples of Christ right along with the men. Even so, that is the interpretation many choose to accept.

10. Paul broke with his own Jewish tradition by instructing women at the same time as men. He spoke directly to them,

instead of relaying his teaching through their husbands or other male authorities. What Paul did is exactly what Jesus did. We also saw in earlier chapters of this book how Jesus chose a woman as his first post-resurrection apostle (one sent out to proclaim the Gospel) and how Paul commended numerous women as church leaders and teachers. Is it realistic to think that all the women whose ministries Paul highlighted were exceptions to his own rule; that women were really intended by God to sit quietly in Christian gatherings and not participate?

11. This is a good section of Scripture to read slowly and carefully. In verse 11, for instance, there are two key words, one often translated as "silence" and the other as "submission." The first is from the Greek word "hésuchia," which means "quietness." This word supports the idea of sitting calmly in a state of inner tranquility; it does not mean to be "speechless."

12. The word "submission" is translated from "hupotage." It comes from a root meaning to "willingly submit." This reinforces Paul's teaching that he wants the women of Ephesus to willingly submit to those who are qualified to teach them.

13. Some say that Jesus did not choose any women to be among his 12 apostles and, therefore, none should be chosen as elders, church leaders or teachers of men. One problem with this argument is that Jesus never chose any Gentiles to be apostles. To be consistent, this argument should lead us to conclude that only Jewish men are qualified to lead and teach in our churches. No one says that. Gentiles (and women) were clearly involved with the church from its early days and the Gospel of Luke is written by a Gentile physician of the same name. And, of course, we can't ignore the women who were involved as leaders and teachers in the early church.

14. In verse 12, Paul writes that he does not permit (or is not allowing) a woman to teach or assume authority over a man.

Again, if this is intended as a permanent rule for the universal church, Paul is contradicting his own behavior. More likely, he is speaking to an Ephesian church, which — at the time of Paul's letter — has been troubled by chaos and false doctrines for at least a decade.

15. *"Assume authority"* is also interesting. Paul selects a very specific Greek word, "authentein," that does not appear anywhere else in the Bible. The word is used in Greek literature to emphasize an assumed authority or one that dominates. It appears Paul is talking about women who assume an authority that is not theirs to take. Our job is to discern how — or if — Paul's words apply today.

16. Paul's references to Genesis in verses 13-15 are cause for more debate. Is Paul asserting that Adam was designed to lead Eve because he was created first or is Paul dealing with a false doctrine in Ephesus, one that mixes mythology about Artemis with the story of Eve and turns Eve into the creator of Adam? This and other possibilities are discussed in Chapter 5.

17. It is likely that in verses 13-15, Paul wants to be sure Christ followers do not mix biblical truth with mythological stories. The most frequent cause of death for women was childbirth. Artemis was thought to protect women during birth. If verse 15 is read as "women will be kept safe during childbearing," it fits Paul's desire to refute false doctrines infecting the Ephesian church. He points women back to Jehovah as their protector, rather than Artemis, who traditionally had that role in Ephesus.

18. I believe the most important question concerning 1 Timothy 2:8-15 is this: Should these much-debated verses be used as a foundation for arguing that women should never teach or lead men in our churches or is it better to focus on how Jesus and Paul actually worked with women as leaders and teachers?

Appendix I
Why trust Genesis?

James G. Murphy's commentary

In his book, *A Critical and Exegetical Commentary on the book of Genesis*, James G. Murphy writes about the theory some have posited that Moses was simply one of the authors of Genesis. He says that while the styles do seem to vary within Genesis, it is no more than is to be expected if the same author tailors the style to the subject matter.

His conclusion is that, "It cannot be demonstrably or even probably ascribed to a medley of passages from different authors … An ancient writing, purporting to be continuous and handed down to us as the work of one author, should be received as such unless we have good and solid reasons for the contrary. The Pentateuch is a book exactly of this description, continuous in its form and coming down to us as the work of Moses, in the main." (The first five books of the Old Testament are all attributed to Moses. Together, they are called "The Pentateuch," which means "five books" or "five scrolls.")

Holman's Study Bible

The *Holman Study Bible* says, "Some radical critics have denied the possibility of God's supernatural involvement in history and questioned the trustworthiness of the history found in the Pentateuch. Yet any adequate view of the Pentateuch must recognize Moses' … historical reliability.

"Deuteronomy, the last book of the Pentateuch, was composed ... just before his death (Deut. 31:2, 9, 24). Genesis, Exodus and Leviticus, however, could have been penned up to 38 years earlier. This (timing) is particularly appropriate because God had already informed Moses that he would not live to cross the Jordan and participate in the conquest and settlement of Canaan (Numbers 20:10-13; 27:12-14).

"It was thus urgent that he bequeath to his people the legacy of divine revelation – the Pentateuch – that the Lord had entrusted to him. The inspired prophet had to address any questions they had about their origins, purpose and destiny then and there. The date of the final form of the Pentateuch as it came from Moses' hand is about 1400 B.C., forty years after the exodus."

Jamieson writes about the Pentateuch

Robert Jamieson, in his well-known *Introduction to the Pentateuch and Historical Books*, says, "That Moses did keep a written record of the important transactions relative to the Israelites is attested by his own express affirmation ....

"First, there are the repeated assertions of Moses himself that the events which checkered the experience of that people were written down as they occurred (Exodus 24:4-7; 34:27; Numbers 33:2). Secondly, there are the testimonies borne in various parts of the later historical books to the Pentateuch as a work well known and familiar to all the people (Joshua 1:8; 8:34; 23:6; 24:26; 1 Kings 2:3, etc.).

"Thirdly, frequent references are made in the works of the prophets to the facts recorded in the books of Moses (compare Isaiah 1:9 with Genesis19:1; Isaiah 12:2 with Exodus 15:2; Isaiah 51:2 with Genesis 12:2; etc. (There are many additional such examples in the Old Testament.) Fourthly, the testimony of Christ and the apostles is repeatedly borne to the books of Moses

(Matthew 19:7; Luke 16:29; 24:27; John1:17; 7:19; Acts 3:22; 28:23; Romans 10:5).”

Can we trust the modern book?

Jamieson writes: “An important question arises as to whether the books which compose it (the Pentateuch) have reached us in an authentic form.” He answers by noting that numerous copies of the Pentateuch existed early on to meet the needs of religious leaders and teachers. The existence of so many copies helped preserve the integrity of “The Book of the Law.”

Besides this, there are other reasons to conclude that the Pentateuch we have today is the same as what was used in ancient times. As Jamieson writes, one is “the discovery in the reign of Josiah of the autograph copy which was deposited by Moses in the ark of the testimony (2 Kings 22).

“The second is the schism of the Samaritans, who erected a temple on Mount Gerizim and who, appealing to the Mosaic law as the standard of their faith and worship equally with the Jews, watched with jealous care over every circumstance that could affect the purity of the Mosaic record.” Writing in 1871, Jamieson concludes, “There is the strongest reason, then, for believing that the Pentateuch, as it exists now, is substantially the same as it came from the hands of Moses.

“The appearance of a later hand, it is true, is traceable in the narrative of the death of Moses at the close of Deuteronomy and some few interpolations, such as inserting the altered names of places, may have been made by Ezra, who revised and corrected the version of the ancient Scriptures. But, substantially, the Pentateuch is the genuine work of Moses.”

The Dead Sea Scrolls add another layer of proof

When the Kings James translators were working on their "modern" translation of the Old Testament in 1604-1611, the earliest Hebrew text available to them was from 1100 A.D. In 1947, caves were found near the Dead Sea that eventually yielded more than a thousand manuscripts dating back to at least 68 A.D. Included were copies of every book of the Old Testament except Esther.

When scholars compared the Hebrew Old Testament (OT) from 1100 A.D. with the OT manuscripts from 1,000 years earlier, they found them to be virtually identical.

These ancient texts, along with thousands of texts and fragments of texts from other sources, provide overwhelming proof that the Bible we have today contains the same OT text frequently quoted by Jesus and his apostles.

Regarding Jesus, in 1991 more of these Dead Sea scrolls were released to the public for the first time. Among them was one that refers directly to the crucifixion of Jesus.

Appendix II
What I believe

This book contains my views about a number of Bible verses that influence male-female relationships, including how marriages and church organizations are meant to be structured. Because what I've written is a mix of scholarship and research-based opinion – as are most Bible commentaries – it seems appropriate to tell you as openly and clearly as possible my underlying beliefs about God and the Bible.

After decades of study, prayer, meditation and experience as a Christ follower, this is what I believe:

1. God is eternal and omniscient. He knows the past, the present and the future. This means He knew the science available to people at the time Genesis was written, the science that would be available in the time of Jesus and the science that is available now. If God is the original scientist, as I believe, He could have explained string theory in Genesis and put thousands of modern scientists out of work. He didn't do that. He left almost all the "how" of creation to be discovered by human scientists. (Physicists describe string theory as an attempt to find one theory that unites these forces of nature: electromagnetism, gravity and the strong and weak nuclear forces.)

2. God is the keeper and teller of truth. Because God does not change, His truth does not change from generation to generation or situation to situation. What we humans think is true most certainly changes, because each generation and each special interest group insists on discovering its own truth.

3. God gave us the Bible. It uses a number of literary forms to present us with accurate information about our Creator, ourselves and the world we live in. These forms include poetry, song, metaphor, historical narrative and parable.

4. The Bible is intended as a book for all times: ancient, modern and future. It can never be out of date.

5. The Bible tells us what we need to know. It does not always tell us all we would like to know. Some questions cannot be answered with 100 percent certainty based on what God has revealed thus far.

6. Before God allowed His book (the Bible) to be published, He "fact-checked" the authors who told His story. There is absolutely zero chance that this all-knowing God, who does everything far better than any of His created beings can possibly imagine, made the error of not making sure that the first chapters of His book are factually accurate.

7. The Bible can be trusted. All of us who attempt to explain what it says cannot. We are subject to our humanity, which introduces biases and other errors. This is why it is so important that each Christ follower takes responsibility for her or his own spiritual growth. We benefit most by learning to become "self-feeders," people who take the time to learn what the Bible says by reading it, thinking about it, praying about what we've read, talking to others in our faith communities and by using the research tools available to us (Hebrew and Greek dictionaries, historical records, archaeological findings, maps, commentaries and so on).

8. The Bible was written by God's people for God's people. It was never intended to be studied, interpreted and understood exclusively by scholars and religious professionals.

9. Modern scholars can be very bright and very wrong in how they interpret Genesis. For instance, I find it difficult to take seriously theories based on the proposition that God allowed an author, or authors, to open His Bible with a series of untrue stories (myths) or that He would allow them to make the truth so obscure that it was not available until these modern times. Some current theories depend on one or both of these ideas.

10. It is enough for me to know that God is the source of all love and He is in control, even when I can't see His presence or I am struggling to understand His purpose.

For a free teacher / discussion leader's guide,
go to www.snopublishing.com

CPSIA information can be obtained
at www.ICGtesting.com
Printed in the USA
FSHW021902050919
61611FS

9 780578 525358